Communications
in Computer and Information Science 502

More information about this series at http://www.springer.com/series/7899

Shiyong Zhang · Ke Xu
Mingwei Xu · Jie Wu
Chengrong Wu · Yiping Zhong (Eds.)

Frontiers in Internet Technologies

Third CCF Internet Conference of China,
ICoC 2014
Shanghai, China, July 10–11, 2014
Revised Selected Papers

 Springer

Editors
Shiyong Zhang
Fudan University
Shanghai
China

Ke Xu
Department of Computer Science
Tsinghua University
Beijing
China

Mingwei Xu
Tsinghua University
Beijing
China

Jie Wu
Fudan University
Shanghai
China

Chengrong Wu
Fudan University
Shanghai
China

Yiping Zhong
Fudan University
Shanghai
China

ISSN 1865-0929   ISSN 1865-0937 (electronic)
Communications in Computer and Information Science
ISBN 978-3-662-46825-8   ISBN 978-3-662-46826-5 (eBook)
DOI 10.1007/978-3-662-46826-5

Library of Congress Control Number: 2015937939

Springer Heidelberg New York Dordrecht London

Printed on acid-free paper

Springer-Verlag GmbH Berlin Heidelberg is part of Springer Science+Business Media
(www.springer.com)

Preface

As the flagship conference organized by the Internet Technical Committee of China Computer Federation, the Third Internet Conference of China (CCF ICoC 2014) was hosted by Fudan University in Shanghai, July 10–11, 2014. The conference focused on the latest advances in research on Internet-related theory and technology.

ICoC 2014 invited authors to submit full papers representing original, state-of-art, un-published research work in areas of Internet communication and computing. Topics include but not limited to the following areas: software defined network, network security, future Internet architecture, Internet application, network management, network protocols and models, wireless network, sensor networks.

ICoC 2014 received 94 submissions, each submission was evaluated by at least three reviewers. After extensive peer-review process involving more than 31 reviewers, 55 papers were accepted including in Chinese and English. Among them, 10 manuscripts were finally selected for inclusion in these proceedings. ICoC will continue to be one of the most respected conferences for researchers working on networks around the world.

July 2014

Shiyong Zhang
Ke Xu
Mingwei Xu
Jie Wu
Chengrong Wu
Yiping Zhong

Organization

The Third CCF Internet Conference of China

—CCF ICoC 2014—

Shanghai, China

July 10–11, 2014

Hosted by

China Computer Federation

Organized by

Internet Technical Committee of the China Computer Federation

Fudan University

Edited by

Shiyong Zhang, Ke Xu, Mingwei Xu, Jie Wu,
Chengrong Wu, Yiping Zhong

Organizers

General Chair

Shiyong Zhang   Fudan University, China

Program Chairs

Mingwei Xu   Tsinghua University, China
Jie Wu   Fudan University, China

Program Vice Chairs

Jun Bi   Tsinghua University, China
Zhigang Sun   National University of Defense Technology, China

Publication Chairs

Ke Xu   Tsinghua University, China
Yiping Zhong Fudan University, China

Organization Chairs

Xin Wang   Fudan University, China
Chengrong Wu Fudan University, China

Program Committee

Baokang Zhao	National University of Defense Technology, China
Chengchen Hu	Xi'an Jiaotong University, China
Chengrong Wu	Fudan University, China
Chunhe Xia	Beihang University, China
Dan Li	Tsinghua University, China
Deke Guo	National University of Defense Technology, China
Dongliang Xie	Beijing University of Posts and Telecommunications, China
Fangming Liu	Huazhong University of Science and Technology, China
Fenglin Qin	Shandong University, China
Fu Chen	Beijing Foreign Studies University, China
Fucai Zhou	Northeastern University, China
Guorong Xiao	Guangdong University of Finance, China
Had Dai	The Sixty-first Research Institute of PLA, China
Hao Ma	Peking University, China
Hejun Li	Huawei Technology Co., Ltd., China
Hua Li	Inner Mongolia University, China
Huajun Chen	Zhejiang University, China
Hui Tian	Huaqiao University, China
Guang Cheng	Southeast University, China

Jian Cui	Peking University, China
Jian Gong	Southeast University, China
Jianping Zeng	Fudan University, China
Jianping Wu	Tsinghua University, China
Jianxin Wang	Central South University, China
Jin Zhao	Fudan University, China
Jing Dong	North China Institute of Computing Technology, China
Jinsong Wang	Tianjin University of Technology, China
Junzhou Luo	Southeast University, China
Kan Li	Beijing Institute of Technology, China
Ke Xu	Tsinghua University, China
Libing Wu	Wuhan University, China
Liehuang Zhu	Beijing Institute of Technology, China
Limin Sun	Institute of Software Chinese Academy of Science, China
Lisheng Huang	University of Electronic Science and Technology, China
Min Yang	Fudan University, China
Ming Chen	PLA University of Science and Technology, China
Mingwen Wang	Jiangxi Normal University, China
Ping Chen	Peking University, China
Pei Zhang	Peking University, China
Renyi Xiao	National Natural Science Fund Committee, China
Rui Xie	Shanghai Jiao Tong University, China
Shiyong Zhang	Fudan University, China
Wei Li	Xi'an Jiaotong University, China
Wenlong Chen	Capital Normal University, China
Wenyong Wang	University of Electronic Science and Technology, China
Xiaofeng Wang	National University of Defense Technology, China
Xiaohong Huang	Beijing University of Posts and Telecommunications, China
Yongfeng Huang	Tsinghua University, China
Xin Wang	Fudan University, China
Xinbing Wang	Shanghai Jiao Tong University, China
Xingwei Wang	Northeastern University, China
Xiushuang Yi	Northeastern University, China
Yan Ma	Beijing University of Posts and Telecommunications, China
Yaohui Jin	Shanghai Jiao Tong University, China
Ying Liu	Tsinghua University, China
Yingyou Wen	Northeastern University, China
Yixin Zhao	Shanhaishu Technology Co. Ltd., China
Yong Cui	Tsinghua University, China

Yong Tang   University of Electronic Science and Technology, China

Yong Xu   South China University of Technology, China

Yu Jiang   Heilongjiang University, China

Yu Xiang   University of Electronic Science and Technology, China

Yueping Cai   Chongqing University, China

Yunlei Zhao   Fudan University, China

Yuqing Zhang   National Computer Network, China

Zhengtao Yu   Kunming University of Science and Technology, China

Zhenpeng Liu   Hebei University, China

Zhitang Li   Huazhong University of Science and Technology, China

Zhongcheng Li   ICT, the Chinese Academy of Sciences, China

Zili Zhang   Southwestern University, China

Contents

Multi-Constrained Multi-Path Routing
for Server-Centric Data Center Networks

Kun Qian, HuanZhao Wang, ChengChen Hu$^{(\boxtimes)}$, Che Zhang,
and Yadong Zhou

MOE Key Lab for Intelligent Networks and Network Security,
Xi'an Jiaotong University, Xi'an, China
huc@ieee.org

Abstract. Server-centric data center architecture has been proposed
to provide high throughput, scalable construction and error tolerance
with commodity servers and switches for cloud data centers. To fully
utilize those advantages of server-centric data center, an effective routing algorithm to find high quality multiple paths in Server-centric network is needed. However, current routing algorithms cannot achieve this
completely: (1) the state-of-art routing algorithms in server-centric data
center just consider hop count when selecting paths; (2) traditional multi-
constraint QoS routing algorithms only find one feasible path and are
usually switch-oriented; (3) present multi-path algorithms cannot guarantee the performance of the founded paths. In this paper, we propose
a multi-constrained routing algorithm for server-centric data centers,
named Server-Centric Multi-Constrained Routing Algorithm (SCRAT).
This algorithm exploits the topology features of the Server-Centric data
center to decrease the algorithm complexity and returns optimal and
feasible paths simultaneously. In simulations, SCRAT has a very high
probability (more than 96 %) to find the exact optimal path, and the cost
of the optimal path found in SCRAT is about 10 % less compared with
path found in previous TS_MCOP. Compared with previous MPTCP,
SCRAT reduces the path delay by 18 % less and increase the bandwidth
by 20 %.

1   Introduction

In recent years, Data Centers (DC) has been widely employed to fulfill the
increasingly demanding requirements for a variety of business needs [1]. Enter-
prises, service providers, and content providers rely on data and resources in
their data centers to run business operations, deliver network services and distribute revenue-producing content [2]. Data Center Networking (DCN) is an
important part of any modern data center, which must deliver high reliability

This paper is supported by the 863 plan (2013AA013501), the National Science
and Technology Major Project (no. 2013ZX03002003-004), the NSFC (61272459,
61221063, 61170245), Research Plan in Shaanxi Province of China (2013K06-38),
the Fundamental Research Funds for Central Universities.

© Springer-Verlag Berlin Heidelberg 2015
S. Zhang et al. (Eds.): ICoC 2014, CCIS 502, pp. 1–15, 2015.
DOI: 10.1007/978-3-662-46826-5_1

and satisfied performance. However, in the current state, it is observed that the network is a bottleneck to computation [3], after careful analysis on the collected data from a large cloud service data center. Efficient routing inside a data center becomes one of the essential and challenging parts of DCN due to the following two reasons. First, the traffic exchanges among the servers in a data center dominates the traffic of a data center. A recent measurement reported the ratio of traffic volume between servers inside a data center to the traffic entering/ leaving the data center to be 4:1 [4]. Second, the scale of the data center grows really fast and it is expected to hold hundreds of thousands of servers in a single data center. In order to interconnect such a large number of servers with commodity switches and servers, Server-Centric Data Center (SCDC) is proposed [5,6]. In SCDC servers are equipped with multiple network interfaces and act not only as end hosts but also as relay switches for multi-hop communications. Although SCDC achieves architectural advantages, its routing algorithms contain limitations. First, state-of-art routing algorithms for SCDC are topology dependent. A specific routing algorithm is only designed for the specific topology (called original routing algorithm). For example, the original routing algorithm for DCell cannot work on other SCDC topologies like BCube. Second, all the original routing algorithms use hop count as routing metric. Without taking path quality into consideration, routing algorithms cannot guarantee satisfied performance for diverse applications in DCNs.

To effectively utilize high performance routing path, general multi-constrained QoS routing algorithms are widely investigated in the context of traditional network, which control traffic of the whole network by adjusting the number of flows through routers and switches, e.g., Multi-Constrained Path problem (MCP) [7], Multi-Constrained Shortest Path (MCSP) [8], Multi-Constrained Optimal Path problem (MCOP) [9], etc. However, all these solutions only calculate one path for an original destination pair and only focus on routings for routers. In addition, these algorithms originally designed for arbitrary topology and no optimizations are considered leveraging the topology characteristics of SCDC. In fact, the performance of the network routing can be significantly improved by exploiting the unique features of SCDC.

In order to overcome the aforementioned limitations and fully utilize multiple paths in SCDC, this paper aims to solve the so-called Multi-Constrained Multi-Path Problem (MCMP), which finds out an optimal path and other sub-optimal paths for routing under multi-constraints. To the best of our knowledge, it is the first time to introduce this problem in the context of SCDC to find optimal routing paths, which is different from finding only multiple paths in DCNs done by previous work. In this paper, we propose Server-Centric Multi-Constrained Routing AlgoriThm (SCRAT) to solve the MCMP problem, which finds feasible paths from source to destination under multi-constraints simultaneously. We utilize the characteristics of SCDC to decrease the complexity of algorithm and propose a specific Multi-Constrained QoS Routing method to weight the cost of links in searching optional paths. Simulations have demonstrated that SCRAT performs much better than original routing algorithm in SCDC.

Specifically, the proposed SCRAT has the following technical merits.

First, SCRAT uses multi-constraints to find out multiple paths with high quality simultaneously. As a result, SCRAT provides an efficient methodology to solve MCMP problem, which is crucial to spread traffic in SCDC. And multiple paths found in SCRAT ensure better available bandwidth and server-to-server throughput than the existing multi-path routing algorithms.

Second, we take topology characteristics of SCDC into consideration when we design SCRAT. As a result, SCRAT makes the relaxation progress more efficiently and decreases the complexity of algorithm and increases the algorithm's accuracy. Compared with present MCOP algorithms that ignore the characteristics of SCDC, SCRAT has a better performance to find the global optimal paths.

Third, SCRAT is a general method for SCDC and can be employed for all the SCDCs topologies, which is an advance over the original SCDC routing algorithms only working for a specific topology.

The rest of this paper is organized as follows. Section 2 overviews existing routing algorithms in Server-Centric network and Multi-Constrained algorithms. Section 3 works out the way to calculate weight vector and cost, and lists some definitions that will be used in this paper. Section 4 describes our SCRAT. Section 5 gives two sets of simulations to evaluate the performance of algorithm. Finally, Sect. 6 concludes the paper.

2   Related Work

Server-Centric Data Center Network is widely researched around the world. In [10], authors mentioned 5 main disadvantages in traditional data center network, such as no performance isolation, limited management flexibility etc. And the solutions to all of those issues are crucial to the future development of data center. In order to overcome them, many new network architectures had been proposed along with high efficient routing algorithms. For example: BCube original routing algorithm assigns server addresses according to their position characteristics. This algorithm systematically finds intermediate servers by 'correcting' one digit of previous server address [6]. However, as mentioned before, original server-centric algorithm only works well in unique architecture and almost all of those initial algorithms choose the path according to hop count. Some researches have been done on routing in all kinds of DCs to provide multi-paths [11,12]. However, in [11] the first way is spreading load by choosing path randomly. It is obviously not an effective solution. The article also mentioned another way to find multi-paths using multi-static VLANs. The minimal number of VLANs of this solution exponentially depends on the number of equipment in data center. Setting too much VLANs in data center is very expensive. In [12], the multi-path selecting algorithm in SPAIN is running the shortest path algorithm for k times. However, computing shortest paths just consider the hop-count constraint, which cannot ensure good performance of chosen paths. And in the process of repeating shortest algorithm for several times, a large amount of computations are unnecessary. Multi-path routing algorithm can be designed in a much more efficient way.

In the field of routing in a general network, multi-constrained routing problem is widely researched [9,13,14,16–19]. In order to solve Multi-Constrained QoS routing problems, many algorithms have been proposed. MCP focuses on finding one alternative path. So path selected by this kind of algorithms is just feasible path. MCSP devotes to finding the shortest path under multi-constraints. So it may not balance the cost of network and take full advantage of resources. MCOP is trying to solve the problem that finding the optimal path under multi-constraints. And MCOP problem is the most meaningful problem in this set of issues. In 2002, Korkmaz and Krunz put forward the H_MCOP algorithm [17]. This algorithm has better performance than all previous multi-constraint algorithms. And it can find out feasible path at a very high possibility. Then this kind of problem appealed many people's attention. There are several algorithms improving the performance of H_MCOP, such as TS_MCOP [20], and EH_MCOP [18]. The TS_MCOP was proposed [20], which improved H_MCOP best. Those algorithms work well in finding optimal path. But they do not provide multi-paths. So they cannot be used directly in the context of Server-Centric Network.

In all, present multi-path algorithms in data center are not efficient. And all general multi-constrained routing algorithms do not consider topology characteristics in SCDC and can only provide one feasible path. Neither of them can solve the MCMP problem, which is fairly significant for the performance of SCDC. So we propose a new routing algorithm to solve it.

3   Foundation and Definitions

3.1   Weight and Cost

According to the different characteristics and properties of constraints, they can be divided into the following three categories [21]: additive constraint (e.g. delay, jitter, cost and hop count) multiplicative constraint, (e.g. link reliability and packet loss probability) and concave constraint (e.g. bandwidth). Assume path P has j hops and $w_i(e)$ means the ith weight of edge e. According to the constraints, we proposed the following functions to compute weights of a path:

Additive Constraint: The weight of additive constraint is represented by summing every link's weight together, shown in (1).

$$w_i(P) = \sum_{l=1}^{j} w_i(e_l) \tag{1}$$

where i is the serial number of all additive constraints.

Multiplicative Constraint: By converting logarithm form of multiplicative constraints to additive constraints, the weight can be calculated with (2)

$$w_i(P) = \prod_{l=1}^{j} w_i(e_l) = e^{(\sum_{l=1}^{n} \ln[w_i(e_l)])} \tag{2}$$

where i is the serial number of all multiplicative constraints.

Concave Constraint: Concave constraints mark the limit of path, and can be directly used as boundaries for selecting paths. So, (3) is used to calculate those concave weights.

$$w_i(P) = min\{w_i(e_1), w_i(e_2), ..., w_i(e_j)\} \tag{3}$$

where i is the serial number of all concave constraints.

In order to calculate various constraints in one function, Jaffe [13] used the linear cost function to represent the cost of path, shown in (4)

$$COST(P) = \sum_{i=1}^{k} d_i w_i(P) \tag{4}$$

where $COST(P)$ indicates the cost of path P and d_i is the coefficient of w_i.

This representing method can be used to calculate the cost of path for Dijkstra Algorithm, which are utilized by many former routing algorithms. However, linear function cannot reflect the real constraints very well. In order to fit actual constraints better, nonlinear function (5) was proposed to calculate the cost of path [14].

$$COST(P) = [\sum_{i=1}^{k} [\frac{w_i}{c_i}]^q]^{\frac{1}{q}} \tag{5}$$

when $q \to \infty$

$$COST_\infty(P) = \max_{1 \le i \le k} [\frac{w_i(P)}{C_i}] \tag{6}$$

By (6), we can precisely find out all feasible paths that meet the multi-constrained requirements. If we use (6) to calculate the cost of paths, Dijkstra algorithm is not suitable any more. So we need to work out an algorithm that can calculate cost with nonlinear function.

3.2 Definitions

Definition 1 (Server-Centric Data Center). *In server-centric data center, servers act not only as end hosts but also as relay nodes for multi-hop communications [15]. In SCDC, there are links that connect servers directly and there is no traditional hierarchic switch structure, which may cause bottleneck in whole network. In SCDC each server links to several, not one, servers or switches, which balances the load of overall network greatly.*

Definition 2 (Feasible Path). *Given a weighted network graph $G(V, E)$, where V represents the set of nodes and E represents the set of edges, $n = |V|$ and $m = |E|$. Each edge $e(v_i, v_j)$ has a link weight vector W with components of K link weight $w_k \geq 0$ for all $1 \leq k \leq K$. And the corresponding constraint vector C with K constraints c_k. A path is a sequence with non-repeated nodes $P = (v_1, v_2, \ldots, v_i)$. Since there are different types of constraints, simply adding weights together is unreasonable. A feasible path $P = (v_1, v_2, \ldots, v_i)$ so that $w_k(P) \leq c_k$ for all $1 \leq k \leq K$.*

Definition 3 (Optimal Path). *In all feasible paths from v_i to v_j noting as $P_1, P_2, \ldots, P_l$, we use (5) to calculate the cost of paths. Then the optimal path is the path P_0 satisfied: $COST(P_0) \leq COST(P_i)$ for all $1 \leq i \leq l$.*

Definition 4 (Neighbor Node Pair). *In Server-Centric network, if two servers v_i and v_j are linked directly or they interconnect each other through one switch, (v_i, v_j) are neighbor node pair. If two servers interconnect via another server, they cannot be regarded as neighbor nodes.*

Definition 5 (Neighbor Node Matrix). *In a Server-Centric network with N servers, the neighbor node matrix is a N^2 matrix M_1. Each element $v_{i,j}$ in M_1 contains hop count, weight vector and cost of the neighbor node path that links v_i and v_j together. If v_i and v_j are neighbor node pair, we note down hop count, weight vector and cost in $v_{i,j}$. If v_i and v_j are not neighbor node pair, we note 0 in $v_{i,j}$. If v_i and v_j connect directly, hop count = 1. If v_i and v_j are connected by a switch, then hop count = 2.*

Definition 6 (Path-Length). *In this paper, if v_i and v_j are neighbor node pair, we define the path-length of path (v_i, v_j) to be 1. If v_i and v_j are neighbor node pair and v_j and v_k are neighbor node pair, then there is a path (v_i, v_j, v_k) between (v_i, v_k), and the path-length of this path is 2. Paths with path-length 3, 4 and so on can be defined similarly.*

4   Algorithm Design

In SCDC, all switches are connected to servers directly. If two servers are neighbor node pair but do not connect directly, it is easy to figure out the intermediate switch's ID through the IDs of those two servers. This kind of topology characteristic offers us great favor to simplify our searching strategy. So when designing routing algorithm in Server-Centric network, we should pay more attention on servers instead of switches and find an efficient way to route by servers. If we fully employ the topology characteristic in SCDC, the routing algorithm can be simplified and more efficient.

Furthermore, as mentioned in the definition of SCDC, no hierarchical structure in SCDC and the linkage is quite flexible. So there are more than one shortest path. And the number of paths own the same path-length of shortest path is even larger. As we know, in general network when the load in overall

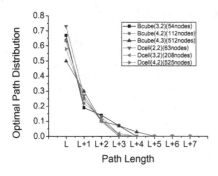

Fig. 1. The distribution of optimal path's path-length in SCDC.

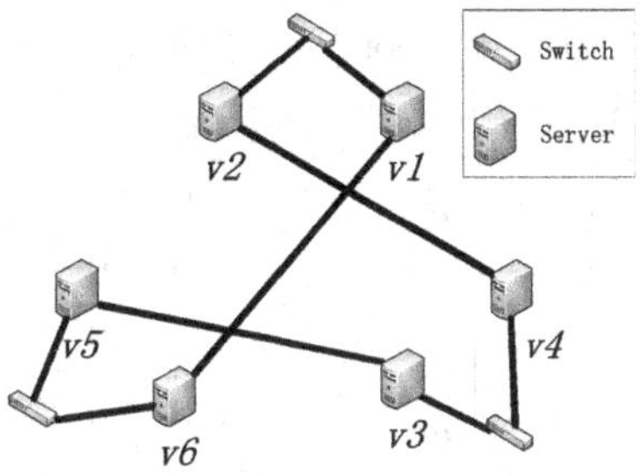

Fig. 2. DCell(2,1)

network is balanced, the shortest path is the optimal path. And in SCDC, due to those topology characteristics of SCDC, the path length of optimal path is very close to the path length of shortest path. We do some research on most widely used SCDC topologies (BCube and DCell). In Fig. 1, we can see that when one feasible path's path-length is bigger than $L + k + 1$, where L represents the path-length of shortest path, it owns fairly low prolixity to become optimal path. This feature guides us to work out a routing algorithm based on the increase of path-length, which is more efficient for SCDC network.

4.1 Algorithm Description

The basic idea of SCRAT is using paths of path-length 1 and paths of path-length N to find paths of path-length $N+1$. SCRAT takes advantage of the fundamental idea of Warshall algorithm to search alternative paths in network. Warshall algorithm is a high-efficiency algorithm to work out the transitive closure of binary relation. However, this algorithm itself can only judge the connectivity of any two nodes in a network, and the complexity of this algorithm is high. In our design, all feasible paths are stored while searching in the graph and the time complexity is decreased successfully by applying the topology characteristics of SCDC.

In order to make the algorithm easily to understand, firstly we use a small network as an example to depict it. In Fig. 2, we build a small DCell model ($n = 2$, $k = 1$) as an example. There are six severs and three switches in this network. And we use four constraints $[c_1, c_2, c_3, c_4]$, in which c_1, c_2 are additive constraints (e.g. hop count; delay); c_3 is multiplicative constraint (e.g. link reliability) and c_4 is concave constraint (e.g. bandwidth). So there are four corresponding weights for any path P. We note the weight vector of P as

$$W_P = [w_1(P), w_2(P), w_3(P), w_4(P)]^T \tag{7}$$

Considering any two servers $v_i, v_j (1 \leq i \leq 6, 1 \leq j \leq 6)$, if (v_i, v_j) is neighbor node pair, then we can calculate the cost of this path with (5). Then we store

Table 1. Generated Matrixes for DCell(2,1)

(a) Neighbor Node Matrix

M_1	v_1	v_2	v_3	v_4	v_5	v_6
v_1	0	$\frac{2}{RI}$	0	0	0	$\frac{1}{RI}$
v_2	$\frac{2}{RI}$	0	0	$\frac{1}{RI}$	0	0
v_3	0	0	0	$\frac{2}{RI}$	$\frac{1}{RI}$	0
v_4	0	$\frac{1}{RI}$	$\frac{2}{RI}$	0	0	0
v_5	0	0	$\frac{1}{RI}$	0	0	$\frac{2}{RI}$
v_6	$\frac{1}{RI}$	0	0	0	$\frac{2}{RI}$	0

(b) Path-Length 2 Matrix

M_2	v_1	v_2	v_3	v_4	v_5	v_6
v_1	0	0	0	$\frac{3\ v_2}{RI}$	$\frac{3\ v_6}{RI}$	0
v_2	0	0	$\frac{3\ v_4}{RI}$	0	0	$\frac{3\ v_1}{RI}$
v_3	0	$\frac{3\ v_4}{RI}$	0	0	0	$\frac{3\ v_5}{RI}$
v_4	$\frac{3\ v_2}{RI}$	0	0	0	$\frac{3\ v_3}{RI}$	0
v_5	$\frac{3\ v_6}{RI}$	0	0	$\frac{3\ v_3}{RI}$	0	0
v_6	0	$\frac{3\ v_1}{RI}$	$\frac{3\ v_5}{RI}$	0	0	0

where RI (related information) contains weight vector and cost value.

hop count and other related information (RI): weight vector and cost value in $v_{i,j}$ of M_1. The result is shown in Table 1(a).

Then we use M_1 to build another vector M_2 that records all feasible paths with path-length 2 and their corresponding information: hop count, weight vector, media servers and cost. Use v_1 as an example. To get paths with the length of two, we first search all neighbor servers of v_1 in M_1. Hence we get v_2 and v_6. We can directly arrive at v_1, v_4 from v_2 and v_1, v_5 from v_6. Removing reduplicative paths and nodes, we get two paths from v_1 with path-length 2: (v_1, v_2, v_4) and (v_1, v_6, v_5). Calculate the weight vectors of the two paths using (1)–(3), then calculate cost by (5). Here we use path (v_1, v_2, v_4) as an example. First two constraints c_1, c_2 are additive constraints, so we choose (1) to compute the weights of first two constraints. So

$$w_1(v_1, v_2, v_4) = w_1(v_1, v_2) + w_1(v_2, v_4) \tag{8}$$

$$w_2(v_1, v_2, v_4) = w_2(v_1, v_2) + w_2(v_2, v_4) \tag{9}$$

The third constraint c_3 is multiplicative constraint, so corresponding weight $w_3(P)$ should use (2) to compute:

$$w_3(v_1, v_2, v_4) = e^{ln(w_3(v_1,v_2))+ln(w_3(w_2,w_4))} \tag{10}$$

Forth constraint is concave constraint, use (3) to calculate the corresponding weight:

$$w_4(v_1, v_2, v_4) = min\{w_4(v_1, v_2), w_4(v_2, v_4)\} \tag{11}$$

The weight vector of path (v_1, v_2, v_4) can be present in the following form:

$$W_{(v_1,v_2,v_4)} = [w_1(v_1v_2v_4), w_2(v_1v_2v_4), w_3(v_1v_2v_4), w_4(v_1v_2v_4)]^T \tag{12}$$

Comparing this weight vector with constraints, if all weights meet multi-constrained requirements, we compute the cost of this path:

$$COST_{(v_1,v_2,v_4)} = \{\sum_{i=1}^{4} [\frac{w_i(v_1, v_2, v_4)}{c_i}]^q\}^{\frac{1}{q}} \tag{13}$$

If any weight of this path excesses the required limitation, we drop this path off. Because all weights are increasing with the increase of hop count, so if a path P_i cannot meet multi-constrained requirement, any other path with a sub-path P_i also cannot meet requirement, too.

In this example, assuming that all available paths meet requirements, we record those paths and its relevant information (hop count, intermediate server, weight vector and cost) into matrix M_2. Similarly, other paths can be calculated in this way, then M_2 is built shown in Table 1(b).

In a similar fashion, with the information from M_1 and M_2, we can build M_3. Then $M_4, M_5, \ldots, M_x$ can be built. Where x indicates the maximum number of path-length that is limited by the QoS requirements. Since the topology of SCDC is very efficient, x is always a small number. For example, in BCube, x can be set as $l + 1$ (l is the port number of a server). All feasible paths between any two servers are available from those tables. We sort them according to their cost, then we can find the optimal path and other alternative paths as well.

The general algorithm is shown in Fig. 3. In the algorithm, $Matrix[u, i, j]$ records all paths and their weigh vectors and costs from v_i to v_j with path-length u. The loop in first line is to search all paths with path-length less than x. The $10th$ line is to pick up all neighbor nodes of v_i. $6th$ and $14th$ lines are calculating the cost of paths using (5). $21th$ line sorts all feasible paths according to paths' cost. Then we can get the optimal path and other sub-optimal paths as well.

4.2   Complexity of Algorithm

SCRAT is an all-to-all routing algorithm. Time complexity of SCRAT is $O((k - 1)^x N)$, where N represents the number of servers; k represents the number of ports on a server and x indicates the given max limitation of path-length. Both k and x are small constants compared with N. The searching cost of prior one matrix is N^2. All $M_2, M_3, \ldots, M_x$ matrix needed to be calculated, so we need to repeat $x - 1$ times. And for each possible path, we need to check all its neighbors, the cost is $k - 1$. In any matrix M_i, for any two nodes, the average number of possible paths is less than $(k - 1)^{i-1}/N$. So the total complexity is $\sum_{i=2}^{x} k(k-1)^{i-1}N \leq k[(k-1)^x - (k-1)]/(k-2)*N = O((k-1)^x N)$. Meanwhile we need a matrix when we store all paths in each path-length. So the spatial complexity of SCRAT is $O(x * N^2)$.

4.3   Proof of Optimality

Proof. In this part, we will prove that if there exists an optimal path satisfying the multi-constrained requirements, SCRAT can guarantee to find it.

Assume that the source server is v_i, and the destination server is v_j. And there is an optimal path meeting multi-constrained requirements, noting it as $(v_i, v_{m1}, v_{m2}, \ldots, v_{mn}, v_j)$. So this optimal path's sub-paths$(v_{m1}, v_{m2}, \ldots, v_{mn}, v_j)$, $(v_{m2}, \ldots, v_{mn}, v_j), (v_{m3}, \ldots, v_{mn}, v_j), \ldots, (v_{mn}, v_j)$ all meet the multi-constrained requirements. Then node pairs(v_i, v_{m1}), (v_{m1}, v_{m2}),...,(v_{mn}, v_j) are all in neighbor node matrix M_1. For the reason that $(v_{m,n-1}, v_{mn})$ and (v_{mn}, v_j) are in M_1, $(v_{m,n-1}, v_{mn}, v_j)$ is in M_2. Due to $(v_{m,n-2}, v_{m,n-1})$ is in M_1, $(v_{m,n-2}, v_{m,n-1}, v_{mn}, v_j)$ is in M_3. And so on in a similar fashion, the path $(v_i, v_{m1}, v_{m2}, \ldots, v_{mn}, v_j)$

SCRAT

```
 1: for (u = 1; u ≤ x; u + +) do
 2:    for (i = 1; i ≤ N; i + +) do
 3:       if u == 1 then
 4:          Find all neighbor nodes {v_{j1}, v_{j2}, ...} of v_i
             from its ID
 5:          if (v_i, v_{jk}) meets all constraints then
 6:             Calculate_COST(v_i, v_j)
 7:             Add[v_i, v_j]into Matrix[u, i, j]
 8:          end if
 9:       else
10:          A = Getsort(v_i)
11:          v_y = any node in A
12:          if [v_y, ..., v_j]is in Matrix[u − 1, i, j] then
13:             if (v_i, v_y, ..., v_j)meets all constraints & No circle then
14:                Calculate_COST(v_i, v_y, ..., v_j)
15:                Add[v_i, v_y, ..., v_j]into Matrix[u, i, j]
16:             end if
17:          end if
18:       end if
19:    end for
20: end for
21: Sort all those available links according to cost
```

Fig. 3. Server-Centric Multi-Constrained Routing Algorithm pseudo-code.

Table 2. Relationship between topology scale and number of nodes

(a) BCube(n,k) Nodes Number

(n,k)	$Nodes$	(n,k)	$Nodes$
$(3,2)$	54	$(6,3)$	2160
$(4,2)$	112	$(5,4)$	5625
$(4,3)$	512	$(6,4)$	14256
$(5,3)$	1125	$(4,6)$	45056

(b) DCell(n,k) Nodes Number

(n,k)	$Nodes$	(n,k)	$Nodes$
$(2,2)$	63	$(6,2)$	2107
$(3,2)$	208	$(8,2)$	5913
$(4,2)$	525	$(10,2)$	13431
$(5,2)$	1116	$(3,3)$	32656

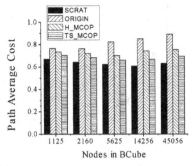
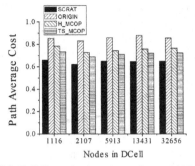

(a) BCube scale increases from 1125nodes (b) DCell scale increases from 1116nodes
(BCube(5,3)) to 45056 nodes (BCube(4,6)) (DCell(5,2)) to 32656 nodes (DCell(3,3))

Fig. 4. The average cost of optimal path selected by different algorithms in different scale of BCube and DCell.

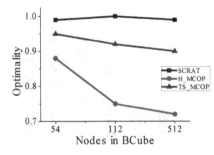
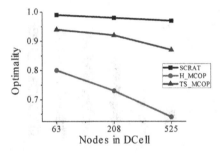

Fig. 5. Optimality is the probability that one algorithm find the exact optimal path under multi-constraint. Because finding the exact optimal path under multi-constraint is an NP problem, we just calculate the exact optimal path in small scale of BCube and DCell.

must be in the matrix M_{n+1}. So SCRAT can guarantee us to find the optimal path if it exists.

5   Simulation

5.1   Simulation Settings

In simulations, we take most widely researched and used SCDC topologies: BCube [5] and DCell [6] as our architectures. The algorithms' performances in other SCDCs are similar. The scale of those two types of topologies is shown in Table 2. Four metrics are selected as multi-constraints: hop count, delay, package loss probability and bandwidth. The hop count between any two servers is fixed due to the structure of network. The bandwidth of all links in topologies are 1Gb.

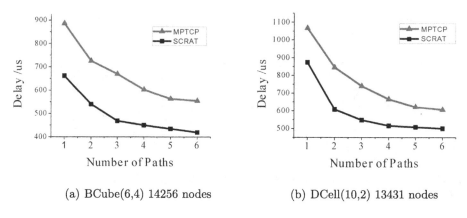

(a) BCube(6,4) 14256 nodes   (b) DCell(10,2) 13431 nodes

Fig. 6. The delay in DCell and BCube using multi-paths computed by SCRAT and MPTCP respectively.

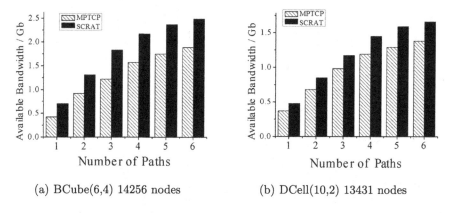

(a) BCube(6,4) 14256 nodes   (b) DCell(10,2) 13431 nodes

Fig. 7. The available bandwidth in BCube and DCell using multi-paths computed by SCRAT and MPTCP respectively.

The initial values of other three metrics are assigned randomly. Specifically the original values of delay, containing waiting time in node and transforming time on link, obey uniform distribution in the interval $(0, 200)$us. Values of package loss probability obey uniform distribution in the interval $(0\%, 5\%)$. The initial values of used bandwidth obey uniform distribution in the interval $(0, 0.6)$ Gb. The constrains generate by $1.5w_k(p)$, where p is the shortest path from source to destination [17]. In each simulation, source and destination are selected randomly and each simulation is repeated for 500 times.

We build two sets of simulations to evaluate the performance of SCRAT. The first set of simulations are to evaluate the quality of the optimal path in SMCMRA. Although SCRAT is a multi-path algorithm, it is also quite important to guarantee the selected optimal path has a high quality. And the second set of simulations are to evaluate the performance of selected multi-paths in SCRAT.

5.2   Simulation Results

Optimal Path Simulations

Average Path Cost: The first simulation compares the optimal path found in SCRAT with the original algorithm, TS_MCOP and H_MCOP. We run each algorithm on different scales of BCube and DCell respectively. And we calculate the cost of path selected in original algorithms, so we can compare them directly. Figure 4 shows the average cost of optimal path found in different algorithms. In those two figures, SCRAT can decrease path cost about 10 % compared with TS_MCOP.

Optimality: In second simulation, we compare the optimality, which is the probability to find the optimal solution if there exists at least one feasible path [20], of SCRAT, H_MCOP and TS_MCOP. Because computing of exact optimal path under multi-constraints is an NP problem and it is almost impossible to work out exact optimal path in large scale of topology, we use small scale of BCube and DCell in simulation. Figure 5 shows the results, where optimality reflects the possibility that the chosen path is the exact optimal path. We can find that SCRAT has the largest possibility to find out the exact optimal path than other algorithms. And with the increase of topology, optimality decreases in a very low rate. So it is convincing that in large scale of topology, SCRAT performs well in finding the exact optimal path.

Multi-Path Simulations. The second set of simulations compare the performance of multi-paths in SCRAT with MPTCP.

Delay of Multi-Path: When we divide one flow into several sub-flows, the overall delay of multiple paths is the maximum delay of all paths. Using multiple paths, the time consumed to pass through links decreases little, but the waiting and processing time in nodes decreases significantly. Figure 6 compares the overall delay of different number of paths selected by SCRAT and MPTCP respectively in BCube and DCell. From the figure, we can find that multiple paths can efficiently decrease the delay to transfer flow. When the number of paths is small, increasing one more path can decrease delay apparently. Compared with paths found in MPTCP, multiple paths found in SCRAT can decrease delay at least 18 %. *Available Bandwidth of Multi-Path:* Figure 7 compares the available bandwidth of different number of paths selected by SCRAT and MPTCP respectively. From the figure, we can find that multi-paths found in SCRAT achieve 20 % more available bandwidth than MPTCP. And with the increase of selected paths, available bandwidth in SCRAT grows faster than MPTCP.

6   Conclusion

MCMP is a very important problem for efficient traffic spreading in SCDC, which has not been solved previously. This paper propose SCRAT to solve the MCMP problem, which leverages the topology characteristics of Server-Centric data center. The algorithm decreases the complexity of the algorithm and simplifies the routing process. Given the path-length, SCRAT can find the optimal path and other sub-optimal paths under multi-constraint. Simulations demonstrate that SCRAT has a very large possibility to find out the exact optimal path and path cost is also lower than the optimal path cost in other multi-constraint algorithm. Additionally, multiple paths found in SCRAT can decrease delay and increase available bandwidth compared with MPTCP.

References

1. Porter, G., Strong, R., Farrington, N., Forencich, A., Chen-Sun, P., Rosing, T., Fainman, Y., Papen, G., Vahdat, A.: Integrating microsecond circuit switching into the data center. In: SIGCOMM, pp. 447–458 (2013)
2. Jain, S., Kumar, A., Mandal, S., et al.: B4: experience with a globally-deployed software defined WAN. In: SIGCOMM (2013)
3. Benson, T., Anand, A., Akella, A., Zhang, M.: Understanding data center traffic characteristics. SIGCOMM Coput. Commun. Rev. **40**, 92–99 (2010)
4. Greenberg, A., Jain, N., et al.: VL2: a scalable and flexible data center network. In: ACM SIGCOMM (2009)
5. Guo, C., Lu, G., et al.: BCube: a high performance, server-centric network architecture for modular data centers. In: ACM SIGCOMM Conference (2009)
6. Guo, C., Wu, H., Tan, K., Shi, L., Zhang, Y., Lu, S.: DCell: a scalable and fault-tolerant network structure for data centers. In: ACM SIGCOMM Conference - SIGCOMM (2008)
7. Kuipers, F., Mieghem, P.V., et al.: An overview of constraint-based path selection algorithms for QoS routing. IEEECommun. Mag. **40**, 50–55 (2002)
8. Reinhardt, L.B., Pisinger, D.: Multi-objective and multi-constrained non-additive shortest path. Comput. Oper. Res. CoR **38**(3), 605–616 (2011)
9. Neve, H.D., Mieghem, P.V.: TAMCRA: a tunable accuracy multiple constraints routing algorithm. Comput. Commun. **23**, 667–679 (2002)
10. Bari, M.F., Boutaba, R., et al.: Data center network virtualization: a survey. IEEE Commun. Surv. Tutor. **15**, 909–928 (2012)
11. Raiciu, C., Barre, S., Pluntke, C., Greenhalgh, A., Wischik, D., Handley, M.: Improving datacenter performance and robustness with multipath TCP. In: ACM SIGCOMM (2011)
12. Mudigonda, J., Yalagandula, P., AI-Fares, M., Mogul, J.C.: SPAIN: COTS datacenter ethernet for multipathing over arbitrary topologies. In: NSDI (2010)
13. Jaffe, J.M.: Algorithms for finding paths with multiple constraints. Networks **14**, 95–116 (1984)
14. Dai, F., Liu, A.: A multi-constrained quality of service routing algorithm based on vector converting. In: WiCom (2009)
15. Chen, K., Hu, C., Zhang, X., Zheng, K.: Survey on routing in data centers: insights and future directions. IEEE Netw. **25**, 6–10 (2011)
16. Mieghem, P.V., Kuipers, F.: Concepts of exact QoS routing algorithms. IEEE/ACM Trans. Netw. **12**, 851–864 (2004)
17. Korkmaz, T., Krunz, M.: Multi-constrained optimal path selection. In: Proceedings of IEEE INFOCOM 2001. IEEE Computer and Communications Societies, Alaska (2001)

18. Wang, S., Wang, H., Li, L.: An enhanced algorithm for multiple constraints optimal path calculation. In: International Conference on Communications, Circuits and Systems - ICCCAS (2004)

19. Puri, A., Tripakis, S.: Algorithms for the multi-constrained routing problem. In: Penttonen, M., Schmidt, E.M. (eds.) SWAT 2002. LNCS, vol. 2368, pp. 338–347. Springer, Heidelberg (2002)

20. Fang, Q., Han, J., Mao, L., Li, Z.: Exact and heuristic algorithm for multi-constrained optimal path problem. In: DAS (2011)

21. Fu, Y., Cheng, X., Tang, Y.: Optimization theory and method. Press of UESTC, Chengdu (1996)

An Efficient Short Null Keys Based Scheme for Securing Network Coding Against Pollution Attacks

Junsheng Wang, Jin Wang$^{(\boxtimes)}$, Yanqin Zhu, and Chengjin Jia

Department of Computer Science and Technology,
Soochow University, Suzhou, China
{20114227046,wjin1985,yqzhu,20134227049}@suda.edu.cn

Abstract. Network coding has gained wide attention nowadays for its significant advantages on many aspects compared with traditional routing mechanism. However, if there are malicious nodes launching pollution attacks by tampering or forging data packets in the communication network, the sink nodes will suffer from failure decoding, together with serious results such as bandwidth wasting, longer transmission delay and increasing computation overheads. The original null keys based pollution detection scheme cannot efficiently defend against pollution attacks when the system has colluding attackers because of high communication overheads. Therefore, we firstly define the concept of complete null space, with the property that no pollution packets can pass its verification. We then propose the idea of partial position detection and design an algorithm to construct short null keys. Secondly, we provide a short null keys based pollution detection scheme with network coding, which has lower overheads compared with the original null keys based pollution detection scheme in composing complete null space. Finally, rigorous theoretical proofs are given to analyze the security of the designed scheme.

Keywords: Network coding · Pollution detection · Null keys

1 Introduction

The idea of network coding has been firstly proposed by Ahlswede et al. in 2000 [1]. Compared with the traditional store-and-forward routing mechanism, network coding allows nodes to encode the received packets to generate new packets and forward the new ones. The theoretical maximum multicast rate can be achieved by using network coding [2].

Recent studies have proved the obvious advantages of network coding in improving network throughput [3], providing data confidentiality [4–8], providing

J. Wang—This work is supported in part by National Natural Science Foundation of China under grant No. 61202378, 61373164. It was also supported in part by China Postdoctoral Science Foundation No. 2013M531402, 2014T70544, and Application Foundation Research of Suzhou of China No. SYG201401.

© Springer-Verlag Berlin Heidelberg 2015
S. Zhang et al. (Eds.): ICoC 2014, CCIS 502, pp. 16–31, 2015.
DOI: 10.1007/978-3-662-46826-5_2

data stream intraceability [9,10], enhancing the robustness of data packets [3,11], enhancing the reliability of the network, facilitating the recovery of redundant data storage [12] and so on. Although the introduction of network coding brings many benefits, the existing of malicious nodes, i.e., attackers, will significantly degrade the system performance in launching pollution attacks [13–17].

Pollution attacks, also known as jamming attacks [18,19] or byzantine attacks [20], belong to active attacks. Malicious nodes tamper or forge the data packets to generate pollution packets and then spread the generated packets into the network. The participation of pollution packets during the encoding of data packets will produce new pollution packets. Consequently, it will result in the diffusion of pollution in the network and further the failure of decoding in sink nodes, without exploiting error detection or correction. Therefore it leads to the waste of bandwidth, the delay in transmission and the increasing of computational overheads.

The null keys based on-the-fly detection scheme is first proposed in [19] to defend against pollution attacks. The null keys used in [19] is referred as *original null keys (ONKs)* and the scheme is referred as *ONKs scheme* in this paper. Besides pollution detection, the scheme further has many other advantages such as good distribution characteristic, low computation overheads during verification, simple to implement, etc. However, since the null keys distributed by the source node cannot compose the complete null space, the obtained distributed null space by colluding attackers will lead to the vanished security of the system.

Based on the *ONKs scheme* proposed in [19], we aim to design an efficient pollution detection scheme in this paper. The main contributions of this paper are summarized as follows:

- We generalize the concept of null keys and propose the concept of complete null space. The existence of complete null space has the ability to put an end to the efficient generation of pollution packets in colluding attackers.
- We propose the ideas of partial position detection and null keys in short length. *Short null key (SNK)* is one kind of short length null keys. We provide the algorithm to generate SNKs, and prove that SNKs have the complete null space.
- We design SNKs based pollution detection scheme with network coding. The scheme introduces the complete null space of SNKs to improve the security level of *ONKs scheme*. *SNKs scheme* reduce the communication overheads which *ONKs scheme* needs.

The remaining parts are organized as follows. Section 2 briefly introduces the related works. Section 3 describes the notations, the network model, the adversary model used in this paper, together with the relevant theoretical descriptions of network coding and null keys for the elaborating of problem. In Sect. 4, our solutions to the problem, the designed SNKs and *SNKs scheme* are presented. Section 5 analyzes the security level of *SNKs scheme*. Finally, we conclude the paper and give prospects in Sect. 6.

2   Related Work

The existing pollution detection schemes can be classified into two categories: the end-to-end error detection or correction schemes [21,22]; and the on-the-fly detection schemes [13–20].

For end-to-end schemes, errors are detected or corrected only at sink nodes. These schemes cost low overheads, but always suffer from detection hysteresis. Therefore, if there are many attackers in the network, or the network that schemes applied to are in large scale, these schemes can not effectively control the diffusion of pollution. The diffusion will lead to the considerable waste of system bandwidth and computing resources.

In order to effectively reduce the waste of network bandwidth in pollution packets transmission, control the diffusion more timely and reduce the influence of pollution attacks, researchers propose the on-the-fly detection schemes. In these schemes, nodes verify the received packets on-the-fly and discard the detected pollution packets. On-the-fly detection schemes are more practical, because it can control the pollution effectively.

Schemes in the second category include the discrete logarithm assumption based homomorphic schemes [14,18,20], the topology based pollution detection and attackers location schemes [16,17], the traditional cryptography based schemes, the lattice theory based schemes and the linear network coding property based null keys schemes [13,15,19].

ONKs scheme [19] utilizes the orthogonal property between the ONKs and the data packets to verify the received packets. ONKs are pre-distributed in the network by network coding. If not all the products of the received coded packet and the ONKs of the node equal to zero, the packet will be treated as a pollution packet. The detail analysis of *ONKs scheme* is available in Sect. 3. In literature [23], we have proposed compressed null keys and designed a compressed null keys based pollution detection scheme to reduce the communication overheads. The compressed null keys proposed are distributed in the same way with ONKs in [19].

Specifically, if the null keys distributed in the network are in network coding mode, the nodes in the scheme need to run discrete logarithm assumption based homomorphism function, proposed in [24], to protect null keys from pollution. Kehdi et al. illustrate experimentally that the *ONKs scheme* with hysteretic null keys, caused by the execution of homomorphism function, can still effectively control the diffusion of pollution packets. However, the prime field, network coding performing on, must be in big size (generally the size of the field is in 256 bit length) for the consideration of guaranteeing the security of homomorphic function [24]. The big size of field will greatly affect the performance of network coding, e.g., it will greatly increase time in encoding and decoding. Moreover, these schemes are not scalable in the network whose nodes have low computational capability to operate in a large finite field, or execute the high computational complexity homomorphism function.

Therefore, compared with previous works in [19,23], the SNKs in the *SNKs scheme* are distributed directly and secretly from the source node to every node to avoid using the high computational complexity homomorphism encryption function. For this reason, the design of *SNKs scheme* is different and more simple to implement.

3 Problem Statement

In this section, we firstly describe the symbols and notations used. Secondly, we give the network model and adversary model. Finally, for the convenience of problem explanation, we provide the relevant theoretical descriptions of network coding and null keys.

3.1 Symbols and Notations

The descriptions of the common symbols and notations used in this paper are listed as follows:

(1) Symbols in bold: the lowercase ones denote vectors or one dimensional arrays, and the uppercase ones denote matrices or sets. (Vector without specification is row vector.)

(2) $|\cdot|$: symbols with absolute value sign denotes the number of elements contained in a vector, one dimensional array, or set.

(3) $rank(\cdot)$: indicates the rank of the matrix.

(4) $row(\cdot)$: indicates the number of rows in the matrix.

(5) $col(\cdot)$: indicates the number of columns in the matrix, vector or array.

(6) $\boldsymbol{x_i}$: given a matrix $\boldsymbol{X}$, $\boldsymbol{x_i}$ denotes the i-th row vector in $\boldsymbol{X}$.

(7) $\mathbb{Z}_n^+$: given a positive integer n, $\mathbb{Z}_n^+$ denotes the set containing all the positive integers that are no bigger than n, i.e., $\mathbb{Z}_n^+ = \{x|1 \leq x \leq n\}$.

(8) $\mathbb{F}_q$: given a prime q, $\mathbb{F}_q$ denotes the finite field in order q. It is also known as the prime field.

(9) $\mathbb{F}_q^n$: given a positive integer n, $\mathbb{F}_q^n = \{[\alpha_1, \alpha_2, \cdots, \alpha_n]|\alpha_i \in \mathbb{F}_q, 1 \leq i \leq n\}$. It is the set containing all the n-dimensional vectors.

(10) $span(\cdot)$: provided that vectors $\boldsymbol{x_1}, \boldsymbol{x_2}, \cdots, \boldsymbol{x_n} \in \mathbb{F}_q^n$ compose a group of vectors, $span(\boldsymbol{x_1}, \boldsymbol{x_2}, \cdots, \boldsymbol{x_n})$ will denote the vector space spanned by these vectors on $\mathbb{F}_q$.

(11) $\boldsymbol{\Pi_X}$: for a vector set $\boldsymbol{X}$, $\boldsymbol{\Pi_X}$ denotes the vector space spanned by the vectors in $\boldsymbol{X}$. For a matrix $\boldsymbol{X}$, $\boldsymbol{\Pi_X}$ denotes the vector space spanned by the row vectors in $\boldsymbol{X}$.

(12) $dim(\cdot)$: denotes the dimension of vector space.

(13) Superscript ^{T}: the transpose of a vector or matrix.

(14) $\boldsymbol{\Pi_X^\perp}$: the orthogonal vector space of $\boldsymbol{\Pi_X}$, i.e., $\boldsymbol{\Pi_X^\perp} = \{\boldsymbol{t}|\boldsymbol{x} \cdot \boldsymbol{t}^T = 0, \forall \boldsymbol{x} \in \boldsymbol{\Pi_X}\}$.

(15) $nullity(\cdot)$: for a vector set $\boldsymbol{X}$ or a matrix $\boldsymbol{X}$, $nullity(\boldsymbol{X})$ represents the dimension of the orthogonal vector space of $\boldsymbol{\Pi_X}$, e.g., $nullity(\boldsymbol{X}) = dim(\boldsymbol{\Pi_X^\perp})$.

3.2   Network Model

This paper concentrates on the multicast communication. The source node is responsible for the distribution of data packets and the providing of detection information. Intermediate nodes are responsible for the verification of received packets and the transmission of data packets. Sink node belongs to a special kind of intermediate node. In addition to have the operations of intermediate nodes, sink nodes still have decoding operations to recover the original data source node transmitted.

Source node divides the original data into data blocks in equal length. All data blocks belong to $\mathbb{F}_q^n$. Every m data blocks compose a data block matrix, denoted by $\boldsymbol{B}$, $\boldsymbol{B} = [b_{i,j}]_{m \times n}, \forall i \in \{1, \cdots, m\}, \forall j \in \{1, \cdots, n\}$. Each row vector in $\boldsymbol{B}$ denotes a data block and $\boldsymbol{b_i}$ denotes the i-th row vector in it.

$\boldsymbol{V}$ denotes the data packet matrix generated according to $\boldsymbol{B}$, $\boldsymbol{V} = [v_{i,j}]_{m \times (m+n)} = [\boldsymbol{I}, \boldsymbol{B}]$, where $\boldsymbol{I}$ denotes the $m \times m$ identity matrix. $\boldsymbol{v_i}$, $\boldsymbol{v_i} \in \mathbb{F}_q^{m+n}$, denotes the i-th row vector in $\boldsymbol{V}$. $\boldsymbol{v_i} = [\overbrace{0,0,\cdots,0}^{m}, \underbrace{1,0,0,\cdots,0}_{i-1}, b_i]$.

Given a vector $\boldsymbol{y}$, if $\boldsymbol{y}$ meets the condition $\boldsymbol{y} \in \boldsymbol{\Pi_V}$, $\boldsymbol{y}$ is a data packet. Although the $m + n$ length vector whose elements are all equal to zero satisfies the definition of data packets, such packet is useless in decoding and will be discarded by nodes.

3.3   Adversary Model

The adversary model established in this paper focuses on pollution attacks. Attackers tamper or forge packets in the network transmission. The scheme designed is above board. Source node during the communication process is believable, and any nodes excluding the source can be potential attackers. Attackers collect information from the data flowing through it, together with the sharing information gained by other attackers for maximally polluting the network.

Given a vector $\boldsymbol{y}$, if $\boldsymbol{y}$ meets the conditions $\boldsymbol{y} \in \mathbb{F}_q^{m+n}$ and $\boldsymbol{y} \notin \boldsymbol{\Pi_V}$ simultaneously, $\boldsymbol{y}$ is a pollution packet. If a node cannot detect out the pollution packet according to its existing information, we say that the node is defeated, i.e., the node is polluted.

3.4   Network Coding and Null Keys

Firstly, we show several relevant concepts of network coding:

Linear Network Coding on Prime Field: Elements in data packets are all represented by elements in $\mathbb{F}_q$. Further, the generated data packet during encoding is a linear combination of the node possed data packets on $\mathbb{F}_q$.

Local Coding Vector: Also called local encoding kernel, is a vector composed by the coefficients node used to encode the possed data packets during network coding.

Global Coding Vector: Also called global encoding kernel, is a vector composed by the coefficients a data packet used when it is represented by the linear combination of $v_1, v_2, \cdots, v_m$.

Kehdi et al. propose that nodes can detect pollution through the orthogonal property of ONKs and data packets [19]. Here are the definitions of null keys related concepts. We generalize the definition of null keys defined in [19]:

Definition 1 *(null keys): The vectors using orthogonal property to verify data packets.*

Definition 2 *(ONK): A kind of null keys. If a vector τ meets the condition that $\tau \in \Pi_V^\perp$, τ is the ONK of Π_V. If all the elements in τ are 0, τ is useless, and will be discarded.*

Definition 3 *(null space): The set of vector spaces spanned by a group of null keys in one kind. Each vector space is spanned by the null keys corresponding to the same verification positions in data packets.*

Definition 4 *(full null space): The largest null space spanned by all the null keys of a single kind.*

Definition 5 *(complete null space): A kind of null space which has the feature that no pollution packets can simultaneously pass the verifications of all the null keys in this space.*

Definition 6 *(distributed null space): The null space spanned by all the null keys source node distributed.*

Following the Definition 2, it is known that $\Pi_V^\perp$ is the full null space of ONKs.

Although the *ONKs scheme* functions well in defending against pollution attacks, and enjoys many advantages, the security level of the scheme is not high enough. Π_Γ denotes the distributed null space in *ONKs scheme*. Since the distributed null space in *ONKs scheme* do not cover the complete null space of ONKs, colluding attackers can easily obtain Π_Γ through the sharing of ONKs they have. (The reason of the partial cover in *ONKs scheme* is available in the analysis of Theorem 2). Consequently, attacker can easily produce pollution packet y,

$$y \in \{y | y \in \Pi_\Gamma^\perp, and\, y \notin \Pi_V\}. \tag{1}$$

y can pass the verification of the ONKs any nodes obtained in the network. It results in the vanished security of the system.

4   Description of *SNKs Scheme*

In this section, we firstly illustrate our design goal and the corresponding solutions of the low security level in *ONKs scheme*. Secondly, we introduce the concept of partial verification positions set (PVPS), and give the definition and the construction algorithm of SNKs. Finally, we describe the SNKs based pollution detection scheme.

4.1 Design Goals

We first give the sufficient condition that there does not exist pollution packets which can pass the verifications of all the null keys in $\boldsymbol{\Pi}_\Gamma$.

Theorem 1. *Given* $\boldsymbol{\Pi}_\Gamma = \boldsymbol{\Pi}_V^\perp$, *no pollution packet exists that can simultaneously pass the verifications of all the null keys in* $\boldsymbol{\Pi}_\Gamma$.

Proof. For $\boldsymbol{\Pi}_\Gamma = \boldsymbol{\Pi}_V^\perp$, we have $\boldsymbol{\Pi}_V = \boldsymbol{\Pi}_\Gamma^\perp$. Only vectors belonging to $\boldsymbol{\Pi}_\Gamma^\perp$ can pass the verification of the whole null keys in $\boldsymbol{\Pi}_\Gamma$. It follows that only data packets belong to $\boldsymbol{\Pi}_\Gamma^\perp$. Moreover, pollution packet $\boldsymbol{y}$ should meet the condition $\boldsymbol{y} \notin \boldsymbol{\Pi}_V$. Hence the proposition is proved.

However, to satisfy condition $\boldsymbol{\Pi}_\Gamma = \boldsymbol{\Pi}_V^\perp$, the number of linearly independent ONKs distributed by the source node is large. To specify it, we introduce the rank-nullity theorem mentioned in [19]. Here is the description of the theorem:

Theorem 2 *[19]. For any* $m \times n$ *matrix* $\boldsymbol{A}$, $m \leq n$, *we have*

$$rank(\boldsymbol{A}) + nullity(\boldsymbol{A}) = n. \tag{2}$$

That is, $\boldsymbol{\Pi}_V^\perp$ is the complete null space of ONKs. For a $m \times (m+n)$ data packet matrix $\boldsymbol{V}$, the number of linearly independent data packets the source distributing is m, while the number of linearly independent ONKs needed to construct complete null space is n. However, practically, n is much bigger than m in the consideration of the introduced overheads of global coding vectors in data packet. As the length of the ONKs is equal to that of data packets, the direct distribution of ONKs to compose complete null space will lead to high communication overhead.

In conclusion, the design goals of this paper are to: (1) improve the security level under the assumption that attackers can obtain the distributed null space; (2) reduce the overheads in introducing null keys.

If we divide each data packet into multiple parts and verify each part by using the orthogonal property of null key, the length of null keys will decrease. Moreover, if such short length null keys exist complete null space, then the communication overhead will be smaller than that of ONKs. In this paper, we design such SNKs based scheme with the mentioned two goals satisfied simultaneously.

4.2 Partial Verification Positions Set (PVPS)

Since the verification positions of null keys decide the structure of null keys and the verification method, we introduce the concept of PVPS. PVPS records the positions extracted during data packets verification. Essentially, there is no order relationship among positions. However, for the convenience of easy presentation, positions are recorded in ascending order, and the set of positions is denoted by vector instead of set. The definition of PVPS is as follows:

Definition 7 (PVPS, S_w): *A vector used to record the positions in data packets, participating in verification. The subscript w is used to distinguish each position set, $1 \leq w \leq u$; u is the total number of different S_w source node distributing. Given a data packet belonging to $\mathbb{F}_q^{m+n}$, $S_{w,k}$ denotes the k-th element in S_w, $S_{w,k} \in \mathbb{Z}_{m+n}^+$, $1 \leq k \leq |S_w|$.*

$\bigcup\limits_{w \in \Omega} S_w$ denotes the union of PVPSs, $\bigcup\limits_{w \in \Omega} S_w = \{S_{w,k} | w \in \Omega, 1 \leq k \leq |S_w|\}$, where Ω denotes the set recording the subscripts of PVPSs.

4.3   Construction of SNKs

Before we define SNKs and introduce the construction algorithm of SNKs, we first describe several related concepts:

The Separated Data Packet $p_{w,i}$: A sub-vector composed by the selected elements in data packet v_i according to S_w. $p_{w,i,k}$, denoting the k-th element in $p_{w,i}$, equals to the $S_{w,k}$-th element in v_i.

Definition 8 (the separated data packet matrix, P_w):
$P_w = [p_{w,1}^T, p_{w,2}^T, \cdots, p_{w,m}^T]^T = [v_{i,S_{w,k}}]_{m \times |S_w|}$, denotes the matrix composed by $p_{w,i}$, $\forall i \in \{1, \cdots, m\}$, as its row vectors.

Definition 9 (S_w of SNKs):

(1) $\forall w \in \{1, \cdots, u - n \bmod u\}$, $S_w = [1, 2, \cdots, m, m + (w - 1)\lfloor n/u \rfloor + 1, m + (w - 1)\lfloor n/u \rfloor + 2, \cdots, m + w\lfloor n/u \rfloor]$;

(2) $\forall w \in \{u - n \bmod u + 1, \cdots, u\}$, $S_w = [1, 2, \cdots, m, m + n - (u - w + 1)\lceil n/u \rceil + 1, m + n - (u - w + 1)\lceil n/u \rceil + 2, \cdots, m + n - (u - w)\lceil n/u \rceil]$.

In the formula, $\lceil \cdot \rceil$ denotes the ceiling of a value, and $\lfloor \cdot \rfloor$ denotes the floor of a value.

Definition 10 (SNK): *A kind of null keys. Given a vector ς_w, if it is the ONK of Π_{P_w}, it is the SNK of Π_V corresponding to S_w. The subscript w represents that the PVPS of the SNK is S_w.*

Full null space of SNKs, Π_V^{snk}: $\Pi_V^{snk} = \{\Pi_{P_w}^\perp | 1 \leq w \leq u\}$. It is a union of all $\Pi_{P_w}^\perp$.

Π_V^{snk} is the complete null space of SNKs (guaranteed by Theorem 4). Algorithm 1 describes the generation of SNKs and data packets. The construction process is similar with that of the ONKs. Note that, when $u = 1$, the SNKs generated by Algorithm 1 will be ONKs.

4.4   SNKs Scheme

Operations of nodes can be divided into five functional modules in the pollution detection schemes. These modules are **Setup, Encode, Distribute, Verify** and **Decode**. Source node functions the first three modules. Intermediate nodes operate the middle three ones. Sink nodes execute the last four ones. We illustrate the *SNKs scheme* through the description of these modules.

Algorithm 1. Generation of SNKs and data packets

Input: Input $m \times n$ data block matrix, $\boldsymbol{B}$;
    size of $\mathbb{F}_q$, q;
    number of parts data packets need to be separated into, u;
Output: Output $m \times (m + n)$ data packet matrix, $\boldsymbol{V}$;
    u matrices storing SNKs, $\boldsymbol{T}_w$, $1 \leq w \leq u$. The first $u - n\bmod u$ ones are $\lfloor n/u \rfloor \times$
    $(m + \lfloor n/u \rfloor)$ matrices, and the remained are $\lceil n/u \rceil \times (m + \lceil n/u \rceil)$ matrices;
 1: $\boldsymbol{V} = [\boldsymbol{I}, \boldsymbol{B}]$;
 2: Set each $\boldsymbol{S}_w$ according to Definition 9;
 3: Set each $\boldsymbol{P}_w$ according to Definition 8;
 4: **for** $(w = 1; w \leq u; w + +)$ **do**
 5:    Find the basis of $\prod \frac{\perp}{P_w}$ (i.e., the basis of the solution space of homogeneous linear
      set $\boldsymbol{P}_w \boldsymbol{X} = \boldsymbol{0}$ on $\mathbb{F}_q$);
 6:    Set the vectors in the basis as row vectors of $\boldsymbol{T}_w$;
 7: **end for**

Setup. Before the communication, source node needs to perform this function module to setup parameters, data packets, SNKs, and so on.

i. Parameters preparing. Determine the value of prime number q, positive integer m, n, u and d. q is the size of $\mathbb{F}_q$. $m = row(\boldsymbol{B})$, $n = col(\boldsymbol{B})$, and $n \gg m$. u is the number of parts data packets separated into, where $1 \leq u \leq n$ and $u|n$. $u|n$ means that n is divisible by u. d is the number of SNKs source node distributing to each node.

ii. Generation of data packets and SNKs. Perform Algorithm 1 to generate data packet matrix $\boldsymbol{V}$ and u matrices, denoted by $\boldsymbol{T}_w, 1 \leq w \leq u$, storing SNKs according to the parameters selected and data block matrix $\boldsymbol{B}$.

Encode. Encoding can be divided into the encoding of SNKs and the encoding of data packets according to the different objects. Only source node needs to execute the first kind.

i. Encoding of SNKs. Given $\boldsymbol{S}_w$, source node randomly selects $|\boldsymbol{S}_w| - m$ coefficients from $\mathbb{F}_q$, denoted by $\alpha_1, \alpha_2, \cdots, \alpha_{|S_w|-m}$. ς_w denotes the encoded SNKs corresponding to $\boldsymbol{S}_w$. We have

$$\varsigma_w = \sum_{i=1}^{|S_w|-m} \alpha_i \cdot \boldsymbol{t}_{w,i}, \tag{3}$$

where $\boldsymbol{t}_{w,i}$ denotes the k-th row vector in $\boldsymbol{T}_w$.

ii. Encoding of data packets. Assuming that a node has l linearly independent data packets, denoted by $\boldsymbol{y}_1, \boldsymbol{y}_2, \cdots, \boldsymbol{y}_l$. These data packets have been verified (the verification of data packets is available in the Verify module listed below). The pollution packets which pass the verification will be seemed as data packets. The node randomly selects l coefficients from $\mathbb{F}_q$ as local coding vector, denoted by $\alpha_1, \alpha_2, \cdots, \alpha_l$, to encode. $\boldsymbol{y}$ denotes the generated data packet. We have

$$y = \sum_{i=1}^{l} \alpha_i \cdot y_i, \tag{4}$$

Distribute. According to the different contents in distribution, it can be divided into the distribution of parameters, SNKs, and the distribution of data packets. Only source node needs to distribute the parameters and SNKs. All nodes in the network need to distribute data packets. The detailed process is as follows:

i. Distribution of parameters and SNKs. Source node needs to distribute the parameters selected in Setup module, and d SNKs to every node. During the distribution process, the communication of these two information should provide integrity. The communication of SNKs should further provide confidentiality. Modern cryptography provides many ways to meet these two requirements, e.g., perform HMAC operations at first and then execute AES symmetric encryption to provide integrity and confidentiality at the same time. These ways are not the focus in this paper, so they are brief and uninformative here. The detailed descriptions of the parameters and SNKs are as follows:

Algorithm 2. The number of SNKs to be transmitted corresponding to each S_w

Input: Input total number of SNKs needed, d;
  number of S_w, u;
Output: Output u length vector storing the number of SNKs corresponding to each S_w, Υ;
1: **for** $(w = 1; w \leq u; w ++)$ **do**
2:    $\Upsilon_w = \lfloor d/u \rfloor$, where Υ_w denotes the w-th element in Υ;
3: **end for**
4: randomly select $d \bmod u$ elements from set $\mathbb{Z}_u^+$ to form set X;
5: **for** each element, denoted by x, in X **do**
6:    $\Upsilon_x ++$;
7: **end for**

---

(1) The parameters are the values of q, m, n, u and d.
(2) Firstly, run Algorithm 2 to determine the number of the SNKs corresponding to each S_w. These numbers will be stored in a u length vector Υ. Υ_w denotes the i-th number in Υ. Secondly, generate Υ_w linearly independent SNKs according to each S_w via the encoding of SNKs listed in Encode module.

Algorithm 2 implements two functions. First, distributes $\lfloor d/u \rfloor$ SNKs to each S_w. Second, for the remained ones in d SNKs, randomly choose $d \bmod u$ PVPSs from the total u S_w. For the selected ones, add Υ_w with one.

In order to inform the node the S_w SNKs corresponding to, the subscripts of the S_w to SNKs will also be distributed together.

ii. Distribution of data packets. Node distributes encoded data packets, generated in the Encode module, to all the downstream nodes of it.

Verify. Every node except the source needs to detect the received parameters, SNKs and packets in communication. As source node does not have upstream nodes, it needs not to perform the verification operations.

    i. Verification of parameters and SNKs. Use corresponding methods in modern cryptography.

   ii. Verification of data packets. If and only if a packet passes the detection of all the SNKs the node gains, can the packet be considered to pass the verification. The steps in using a single SNKs, denoted by ς_w, to verify a packet, denoted by y, are as follows:

      (1) Firstly, select elements from y to construct sub-vector y_w. The elements selected are indexed by S_w.

      (2) Calculate the value of $y_w \cdot \varsigma_w^T$. If the product is not 0, y is a pollution packet.

Decode. Sink nodes can decode and receive the original data packet after receiving m linearly independent correct packets.

Although the *SNKs scheme* described above is performed on prime field, it has no influence for the application of the scheme on Galois field, such as $\mathbb{GF}(2^n)$. Since the calculations on $\mathbb{GF}(2^n)$ are XOR calculations, it accelerates the speed. Moreover, *SNKs scheme* can combine with the scheme in [15]. The split SNKs can further reduce the amount of updated null keys when changes the data block matrix (the details are not the point of this paper).

5 Security Analysis

In this section, we firstly analyze the attack way of malicious nodes. Then, the security level of the SNKs based scheme against random position attack are analyzed. We prove that the complete null space of the SNKs equals to its full null space. At last, we calculate the probability of nodes in composing complete null space.

5.1 Security Against Random Position Attack

During the communication, any transmitted data maybe tampered by attackers. Yet, as the parameters and the SNKs are distributed secretly to each node separately by the source node, their confidentiality and integrity are guaranteed by the existed cryptographic methods. Their security level is beyond the scope of this paper. In this paper, we mainly discuss the attacks on data packets.

    The attacks, in which pollution packets produced according to the SNKs of colluding attackers, are not considered in this paper. Since the null keys belonging to different nodes are concealed from each other, the attackers can hardly speculate the null keys of other regular nodes to gain higher probability of successful attack. Therefore, it launches the random position attack as follows:

Random Position Attack: Attackers produce pollution packets by randomly selecting and modifying the elements in $\mathbb{F}_q$.

It can be seen that any packets belonging to $\mathbb{F}_q^{m+n}$ can be produced by random position attack, that is, this way of attack can produce all possible pollution packets. Note that the SNKs corresponding to Π_V are the ONKs corresponding to Π_{P_w}. The following theorem analyzes the security level single node having against random position attack.

Theorem 3 *[23]. Suppose that a node gets t SNKs $t = \sum_{w=1}^{u} t_w$, t_w is the number of linearly independent SNKs one node got corresponding to Π_{P_w}. Then, the probability that the node is defeated by random position attack is*

$$\frac{q^{m+n-t} - q^m}{q^{m+n}}. \tag{5}$$

Provided that a node gets t linearly independent ONKs, the probability that the node is defeated by random position attack is also equal to $\frac{q^{m+n-t}-q^m}{q^{m+n}}$ [19]. Combining it with the conclusion in Theorem 3, we can see that either we use SNKs to verify the data packets or we use ONKs to verify, the ability of null keys to fight against random position attack is same if given the same number of linearly independent null keys.

In addition, it can be deduced from Definition 9 and Theorem 2 that the total number of linearly independent SNKs corresponding to each S_w in Π_V^{snk} is $\Sigma_{w=1}^{u}(|S_w| - m) = n$. Also the number of linearly independent ONKs in $\Pi_V^{\perp}$ is n. Therefore, in defending against random position attack, SNKs and ONKs have same ability level.

5.2 The Complete Null Space of SNKs

In this subsection, we prove that SNKs exists complete null space.

Theorem 4. *The complete null space of SNKs is Π_V^{snk}.*

Proof. According to Theorem 3, we know that if $t = n$, no pollution packets can pass the verification of all these n SNKs. On the other hand, the null space these n SNKs composing is Π_V^{snk}. Hence, the proposition is proved.

The proved theorem follows that the amount of SNKs in composing complete null space is smaller than that of ONKs. Since these two kinds of null keys both need n null keys to compose complete null space on one side, the length of SNKs are shorter than ONKs on the other hand.

Since each node obtains limited number of SNKs, the keys belonging to a single node can hardly composing complete null space. However, as data packets are transmitted by number of nodes, SNKs belonging to these nodes can hierarchies filter the pollution packets. It is obviously that the easier the null keys composing the complete null space for nodes, the more effectual pollution control ability the pollution detection scheme enjoying.

In this part, we mainly discuss the probability of null keys in composing complete null space among nodes. Before the discussion, we firstly introduce the concepts of matrix $C_{k \times n}$, probability $P_{k,j}$, and the probability of randomly generating full rank square matrix on $\mathbb{F}_q$. Their notations are arranged as follows, and the details are available in [25].

Matrix $C_{k \times n}$: $C_{k \times n}$ is a $k \times n$ random matrix on $\mathbb{F}_q$.

Probability $P_{k,j}$: $P_{k,j} = P\{rank(C_{k \times n}) = j\}$, i.e., $P_{k,j}$ is the probability that the rank of matrix $C_{k \times n}$ is j. Provided $P_{0,0} \triangleq 1$.

Theorem 5 *[25]. The probability of randomly generating full rank square matrix on $\mathbb{F}_q$ is*

$$P_{n,n} = \prod_{0 \le i < n} (1 - q^{i-n}). \tag{6}$$

Equation (6) is a reflection to the linearly independence of randomly generated vectors to some extend.

The Verification Positions Covering Data Packets n/d Times: Provided $u|d$, each node will receive n/d linearly independent SNKs corresponding to each S_w. It is called that the verification positions of these SNKs n/d times covering data packets.

Theorem 6. *Provided that the verification positions cover data packets once time, the probability that the SNKs, belonging to every n/u nodes, can compose the complete null space is*

$$\left(\prod_{0 \le i < n/u} (1 - q^{i-n/u}) \right)^u. \tag{7}$$

Proof. Since the verification positions once time cover data packets, there are n/u SNKs corresponding to each S_w for every n/u nodes.

A_w, $1 \le w \le u$, denotes the event that n/u randomly generated SNKs corresponding to S_w can compose $\Pi_{P_w}^{\perp}$. $P(A_w)$ denotes the probability that event A_w will occur. A denotes the event that the SNKs, belonging to every n/u nodes, can compose the complete null space. $P(A)$ denotes the probability that event A will occur. According to the definitions of A_w and A, we have

$$P(A) = P(A_1 A_2 \cdots A_u). \tag{8}$$

As SNKs corresponding to each S_w are generated by source node via randomly network coding, $P(A_w)$ equals to the probability of randomly generating full rank $C_{(n/u) \times (n/u)}$ on $\mathbb{F}_q$, i.e., equals to $P_{n/u,n/u}$. Following Eq. (6), we have

$$P(A_w) = P_{n/u,n/u} = \prod_{0 \le i < n/u} (1 - q^{i-n/u}). \tag{9}$$

Since SNKs, corresponding to different S_w, composing $\Pi_{P_w}^{\perp}$ act independently. Hence, events A_w, $1 \leq w \leq u$, are independent and identically distributed. We have

$$P(A) = P(A_1 A_2 \cdots A_u) = (P_{n/u,n/u})^u = \left(\prod_{0 \leq i < n/u} (1 - q^{i-n/u}) \right)^u.$$

Provided that the verification positions cover data packets once time, every n/u nodes in the network will receive n SNKs from source node in total. Equation (7) shows the probability these SNKs composing complete null space. Given $n = 160$, $u = 10$, $q = 53$ (a very small prime corresponding to the generally 256 bit q in the schemes that null keys are protected by homomorphism function), the probability, for every n/u nodes to compose the complete null space, is bigger than 80 %. (The value of n, in regular value range of network coding schemes, has little impact on this probability.)

6   Conclusion

This paper concentrates on designing a on-the-fly SNKs based pollution detection scheme. We firstly analyze the ONKs based schemes and show the limitations of these schemes. Then, we generalize the concept of null keys and propose the concept of complete null space. We also propose the ideas of partial position detection, short null keys and provide the algorithm to generate SNKs. We design SNKs based pollution detection scheme with network coding. Through rigorous theoretical proofs, we analyze the security of the *SNKs scheme*. Analysis shows that the security level of our scheme is same with the *ONKs scheme*, and the communication overheads of ours are less than the ONKs scheme to defend against random position attacks.

References

1. Ahlswede, R., Cai, N., Li, S., Yeung, R.: Network information flow. IEEE Trans. Inf. Theor. (TIT) **46**(4), 1204–1216 (2000)
2. Li, S., Yeung, R., Cai, N.: Linear network coding. IEEE Trans. Inf. Theor. **49**(2), 371–381 (2003)
3. Gkantsidis, C., Rodriguez, P.: Network coding for large scale content distribution. In: Proceedings of IEEE International Conference on Computer Communications (INFOCOM), pp. 2235–2245 (2005)
4. Cai, N., Yeung, R.: Secure network coding. In: Proceeding of IEEE International Symposium on Information Theory (ISIT), p. 323 (2002)
5. Bhattad, K., Narayanan, K.R.: Weakly secure network coding. In: Proceeding of the First Workshop on Network Coding, Theory, and Applications (NetCod), pp. 1–6 (2005)
6. Wang, J., Wang, J., Lu, K., Xiao, B., Gu, N.: Optimal linear network coding design for secure unicast with multiple streams. In: Proceedings of IEEE International Conference on Computer Communications, pp. 1–9 (2010)

7. Wang, J., Wang, J., Lu, K., Qian, Y., Xiao, B., Gu, N.: Optimal design of linear network coding for information theoretically secure unicast. In: Proceedings of IEEE International Conference on Computer Communications, pp. 757–765 (2011)
8. Wang, J., Wang, J., Lu, K., Xiao, B., Gu, N.: Modeling and optimal design of linear ntwork coding for secure unicast with multiple streams. IEEE Trans. Parallel Distrib. Syst. **24**(10), 2025–2035 (2013)
9. Wang, J., Lu, K., Wang, J.P., Qiao, C.: Untraceability of mobile devices in wireless mesh networks using linear network coding. In: Proceedings of IEEE International Conference on Computer Communications(INFOCOM mini-conference), pp. 270–274 (2013)
10. Wang, J., Wang, J., Wu, C., Lu, K., Gu, N.: Anonymous communication with network coding against traffic analysis attack. In: Proceedings of IEEE International Conference on Computer Communications, pp. 1008–1016 (2011)
11. Koetter, R., Mdard, M.: An algebraic approach to network coding. IEEE/ACM Trans. Netw. (TON) **11**(5), 782–795 (2003)
12. Dimakis, A.G., Godfrey, P.B., Wu, Y., Wainwright, M.J., Ramchandran, K.: Network coding for distributed storage systems. In: Proceedings of IEEE International Conference on Computer Communications, pp. 2000–2008 (2007)
13. Zhang, P., Jiang, Y., Lin, C., Yao, H., Wasef, A., Shen, X.S.: Padding for orthogonality: efficient subspace authentication for network coding. In: Proceedings of IEEE International Conference on Computer Communications (INFOCOM), pp. 1026–1034 (2011)
14. Charles, D., Jian, K., Lauter, K.: Signature for network coding. Inf. Coding Theory **1**(1), 3–14 (2009)
15. Newell, A., Nita-Rotaru, C.: Split null keys: a null space based defense for pollution attacks in wireless network coding. In: Proceedings of IEEE Communications Society Conference on Sensor, Mesh and Ad Hoc Communications and Networks (SECON), pp. 479–487 (2012)
16. Le, A.: Cooperative defense against pollution attacks in network coding using spacemac. Communications **30**(2), 442–449 (2012)
17. Wang, Q., Vu, L., Nahrstedt, K., Khurana, H.: MIS: malicious nodes identification scheme in network-coding-based peer-to-peer streaming. In: Proceedings of IEEE International Conference on Computer Communications, pp. 1–5 (2010)
18. Gkantsidis, C., Rodriguez, P.: Cooperative security for network coding file distribution. In: Proceedings of IEEE International Conference on Computer Communications (INFOCOM), pp. 1–13 (2006)
19. Kehdi, E., Li, B.: Null keys:limiting malicious attacks via null space properties of network coding. In: Proceedings of IEEE International Conference on Computer Communications (INFOCOM), pp. 1224–1232 (2009)
20. Zhao, F., Kalker, T., Medard, M., Han, K.J.: Signatures for content distribution with network coding. In: Proceedings of IEEE International Symposium on Information Theory (ISIT), pp. 24–29 (2007)
21. Yeung, R.W., Cai, N.: Network error correction. Commun. Inf. Syst. **6**(1), 19–35 (2006)
22. Koetter, R., Kschischang, F.: Coding for errors and erasures in random network coding. IEEE Trans. Inf. Theory **54**(8), 3579–3591 (2008)
23. Wang, J., Wang, J., Zhu, Y., Lu, K.: SNKC: an efficient on-the-fly pollution detection scheme for content distribution with linear network coding. In: Proceedings of International Conference on Embedded and Ubiquitous Computing, pp. 2298–2305 (2013)

24. Krohn, M., FreedMan, M., Mazieres, D.: On-the-fly verification of rateless erasure codes for efficient content distribution. In: Proceedings of IEEE Symposium on Security and Privacy, pp. 226–240 (2004)
25. Zhao, Y.: The probability distribution of the matrix rank on fq and the asymptotic properties of the rank. J. Inf. Eng. Inst. **15**(4), 47–52 (1996)

Mirror Data to the Ceiling: A New Completely Wireless Data Center

Yawei Zhao[1]([⊠]), Honghui Chen[1], Jia Xu[3], Hanlin Tan[2], and Tao Chen[1]

[1] Science and Technology on Information Systems Engineering Laboratory,
Changsha, China
{zhaoyawei09,chh0808}@gmail.com, chentao@nudt.edu.cn
[2] School of Information System and Management, National University
of Defense Technology, Changsha 410073, Hunan, China
hanlin_tan@nudt.edu.cn
[3] School of Computer, Electronics and Information,
Guangxi University, Guangxi 530004, Nanning, China
xujia.neu@gmail.com

Abstract. Traditional data centers, which are based on wired networks, have been installed many years. However, they often suffer from high cost of construction and management. The data-intensive workloads motivate modern data centers to utilize higher-bandwidth networks like 10 Gb Ethernet (10 GbE). Traditional wired data centers, suffering from complex wiring and management, can not always satisfy this requirement. Wireless data centers have some advantages such as economical installing and no worry about wiring. This paper proposes a new completely wireless data center, which has good performance and high fault tolerance to the network failures. We propose a novel data center design including intra-rack and inter-rack architectures. Especially, inter-rack data transmission can be finished by one hop when we transmit data via the ceiling. Data center, built with this methodology, is significantly convenient to be deployed and managed, which avoids the complex wiring and too much material cost. Extensive simulations have been conducted to verify the effectiveness of our proposal. Our novel design of wireless data center outperforms Cayley data center on bandwidth and good fault tolerance as well as reducing hotspot in the network.

Keywords: Wireless data center · Inter-rack communication · Cayley graph

1 Introduction

Nowadays, data centers have become an important computing platform and play an important role for large-scale internet service like Google and Facebook. Traditional wired data center networks are tree-structured and oversubscribed to cut down cost. However, each oversubscribed link is a potential hotspot that hinders some data center applications [1]. This problem can be tackled by utilizing more links, switches, and multipath routing protocols [2,3]. Fat-Tree [4]

© Springer-Verlag Berlin Heidelberg 2015
S. Zhang et al. (Eds.): ICoC 2014, CCIS 502, pp. 32–45, 2015.
DOI: 10.1007/978-3-662-46826-5_3

leverages largely commodity Ethernet switches to support aggregated bandwidth of clusters. PortLand [5] employs a lightweight protocol to enable switches to discover their position, further assigns internal Pseudo MAC addresses to all end hosts and encodes their position in the topology. VL2 [6], using flat addressing, allows service instances to be placed anywhere in the network. In VL2, Valiant Load Balancing is designed to spread traffic uniformly across network paths. Besides, end-system based address resolution is helpful to scale to large server pools, without introducing complexity to the network control plane. However, wired data centers usually lead to large material cost and wiring complexity.

Reference [7] presents HEELLO which is a hybrid architecture with electrical/optical switches. It can significantly reduce the number of switches, cost, and power consumption compared to recently proposed data center architectures. Reference [8] proposes a hybrid packet and circuit switched data center architecture. It augments the traditional hierarchy of packet switches with a high speed, low complexity, and rack-to-rack optical circuit-switched network to offer high bandwidth. These recent efforts improves traditional wired data centers. However, there are many weaknesses. Besides the expensive optical switches, it is challenge to widely install the optical switches replacing existing wired data centers. On the other hand, these research efforts may not improve the performance of exist data centers in a large scale with the optical switches.

Recently, some proposals [9] about wireless data center bring us a new vision. Millimeter wavelength wireless technology is rapidly being developed. Spectrum between 57–64 GHz, known as 60 GHz band, is available world-wide for unlicensed use. Based on standard 90 nm CMOS technology, new 60 GHz transceiver [10,11] makes it possible to realize such channels with low cost and high power efficiency (<1 W). Directional (25–60 wide) short-range beams enable a large number of transmitters to simultaneously communicate with multiple receivers in tight confined spaces. The indoor 60 GHz technologies such as 802.11 ad [12] target at short range of 10 m and utilize directional antennas. With directional antennas, 60 GHz links can support multi-Gbps rates over distances of several meters. Some wires in the data centers can be replaced with wireless links in the transmission range of 60 GHz channel. It is the origin idea for our research.

Compared to the Cayley data center, our proposal significantly exhibits higher bandwidth by reducing the number of hops in the wireless link, and better extensibility. Cayley data center exhibits strong fault tolerance which outstandingly outperforms for the inter-rack communication in our proposal. In summary, this paper makes three contributions.

- We propose a novel completely wireless system-level data center architecture. The novel architecture design has good performance and reduce the worry of wiring and much material cost.
- A corresponding geographic routing protocol is proposed, and it is proved to be simple but effective, especially for the inter-rack communication.
- Extensive simulations are conducted to evaluate the performance of our novel design, which verify the advantages of fault tolerance and load balance.

The rest of the paper is organized as follows. In Sect. 2, we presents related preliminary and design rationale. System architecture and incorporated routing protocol is proposed in Sect. 3. In Sect. 4, extensive simulations have been done for evaluate the performance of the novel wireless data center design. We wrap up with a discussion in Sect. 5, and related work in Sect. 6. Finally, we conclude our work in Sect. 7.

2   Preliminary and Design Rationale

In this section, we propose a novel completely wireless data center architecture, which utilize the plane reflection principle and 60 GHz communication technology to achieve the goal of high bandwidth and good fault tolerance. We design two wireless communication models to implement the data transmission between intra- and inter-rack servers.

2.1   Preliminary

Wireless signal propagation is the behavior of radio waves when transmitted, or propagated from one point to another. Radio waves, propagated in the indoor environment, are affected by the phenomena of reflection, diffraction and scattering [13].

Reflection occurs at the surface of an object when the size of object is large compared with the wavelength of the incident wave. When the object is a dielectric, some of the incident energy is transmitted and some is reflected. The amount of power reflected from the surface depends on the complex permittivity of the material, its thickness and surface roughness and the frequency of the incident weave. More details can be referred in [14]. Diffraction occurs when the propagation path between the transmitter and the receiver is obstructed by sharp edge on a surface. The wave length of 60 GHz is about 5 mm. It is rather small in the data center, so the effect of diffraction is ignored. Scattering of electromagnetic energy occurs when the wave is incident on a non-uniform surface which has dimensions that are small relative to the wavelength. Reflection, diffraction and scattering all have influence to the quality of communication, but the reflection is the principal factor.

2.2   Design Rationale

Recently, Cayley data center has good performance for intra-rack communication. As the 60 GHz wireless signal is only transferred in short range, Cayley data center has obvious disadvantage on the inter-rack communication. We propose a novel completely wireless architecture which contains two components including intra- and inter-rack designs.

Intra-Rack Design: The design of intra-rack in Cayley data center is inherited in our proposal. Rack is a basic element in the architecture, and each rack consists of 5 storeys. As illustrated in Fig. 1, 20 servers are placed on a same storey in the way of ring. A server is installed in a prism-shaped container. However, each server contains one transceiver which is responsible for intra-rack communication. This is different from the Cayley data center in which two transceivers are installed in each server.

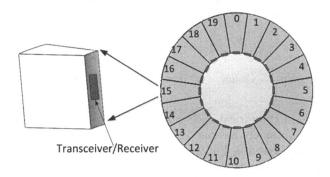

Fig. 1. The design of intra-rack

Inter-Rack Design: The significant difference with Cayley wireless data center is the inter-rack wireless communication design. In Cayley data center, racks connect with neighbors in the way of Cayley graph. However, when a server in one rack wants to transmit data to an another server in other rack, it has to set up a wireless link forward via too many other racks. This brings too much overload to the network, and reduces available bandwidth anyway. What's worse, As the wavelength of 60 GHz radio wave is about 5 mm, it is easy to be blocked by obstacles whose size is larger than 2.5 mm. We think mirror can be helpful to solve these problems. As illustrated in Fig. 2, a mirror is put on the ceiling. Rack r_1 and r_2 are put in the any place of a data center, and servers on the top storey can connect with each other by reflecting the wireless signal to the mirror. Without loss of generality, we can set up the connection between r_1 and r_2 by adjusting the directional antennas to set up a wireless link. This design has two advantages at least. First, if the data center is deployed and the position of a rack is fixed, we can set up the wireless link between any two racks by adjusting the directional antennas. It improves the efficiency of the data transmission and does not reduce the bandwidth of the network. Secondly, complex wiring can be avoided when the data center has to be adjusted.

3   System Architecture and Routing Protocol

Think about the architecture of a rack, we propose cylindrical racks that store servers in prism-shaped containers, because if the volume and bottom area are same, cylinder has larger side area than cuboid, and more servers can be positioned in the rack. In other words, if we put the same number of servers in the

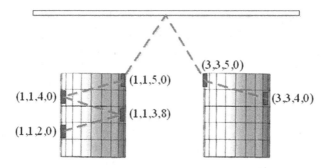

Fig. 2. Ceiling is used to reflect wireless signal.

rack, the servers in cylindrical rack can get better cool service. Every server in prism-shaped containers has one transceiver to communicate with others in the same rack. As showed in Fig. 2, a server can be represented in the form of $(r_x, r_y, s, s*)$. r_x represents the X-coordinate of rack (r_x, r_y), and r_y the Y-coordinate. s represents the storey ID which the server is positioned on, and $s*$ is the label of server ranging from 0 to 19. For each server, it can connect with other 8 servers on the same. If the server is not on the $1st$ storey or $5th$ storey, it can also connect with the same server labels with the upper and lower storeys. For example, if one server is represented as $(3, 3, 3, 0)$, then it has 15 neighbors. These neighbors can be parted in three groups. On the $3rd$ storey, they include servers labeled 8, 9, 10, 11, 12, and on the $2nd$ and $1st$ storey they are same too. Of course, servers on the $1st$ and $5th$ storey only have 10 neighbors. Related routing table is list in Table 1.

Table 1. Server's one hop routing

source server: s	destination server: $s*$
s	$(s + k)\% \, 20(k = 8, 9, 10, 11, 12)$

This design makes sure that server in one rack can set up a wireless link with others within 3 hops. For example, server $(1, 1, 2, 0)$ can transmission data to server $(1, 1, 3, 8)$ immediately, and to server $(1, 1, 2, 1)$ by way of $(1, 1, 2, 10)$, and to server $(1, 1, 2, 5)$ via $(1, 1, 2, 8)$ and $(1, 1, 2, 16)$. This is the base of good fault tolerance for the rack. Related routing algorithm has been designed as Algorithm 1.

Then, think about the architecture of inter-rack. Inter-rack wireless link is necessary to a data center, and essential to fault tolerance for the entire network. Ever rack can set up a wireless link via 20 servers positioned on the top storey. That is to say, if a server on a storey (not the top) wants to transmit the data with servers in other racks, it has to transmit data to the servers on the top storey, and then via the servers on the top storey in the destination rack to reach the destination servers.

Algorithm 1. Intra_Rack_Connection(server s_1, server s_2)

Require: Set up a wireless link between two servers s_1 and s_2 within one rack.

1: $result\_list$.add(s_1); ($result\_list$ records servers on the routing path;)
2: **if** s_1.neighbors.contain(s_2)==$true$ **then**
3:     **for** each server s in the s_1.neighbors **do**
4:         **if** $s.idle == true$ **then**
5:             $result\_list$.add(s);
6:             return;
7:         **end if**
8:     **end for**
9: **end if**
10: **for** $i = 1$ to s_1.neighbors.length **do**
11:     server $s^* \leftarrow s_1$.neighbors(i);
12:     **if** $s * .idle == true$ **then**
13:         Intra_Rack_Connection(s^*, s_2);
14:     **end if**
15: **end for**

As we know, data center has tons of racks which can not communicate with others directly. The wireless signals for data transmission influent each other and do harm to the wireless link. Similar situation should be void. Inspired by the plane reflection principle, we propose inter-rack connection architecture. Servers on the top storey in different racks can connect with each other by the mirror on the ceiling. For example, if server (1, 1, 2, 0) wants to transmit data to server (3, 3, 4, 0), it firstly transmits data to server (1, 1, 5, 0) (other servers on the same storey is also ok.). Server (1, 1, 5, 0) transmits the data to server (3, 3, 5, 0) (others on the same storey is also ok). Eventually the data is transmitted to the destination server (3, 3, 4, 0).

Figure 2 illustrates a planar slice of the geometric communication model we described in the paper. Servers s_1 and s_2 are positioned on racks r_1 and r_2 respectively. Directional antenna is installed on the server to reduce the loss of wireless signals. Wireless transceiver is a recent integrated implementation from Georgia Tech. More details about the transceiver can refer [15]. Based upon Georgia Tech's design [14], the wireless transceiver has bandwidth ranging from 4 to 15 Gbps with less than 10 m communication range. Even though oxygen absorption in the 60 GHz range is seen as a concern in other contexts, but the loss (15 dB/km) is negligible for the typical distances within data centers (less than 10 m). On the other hand, some phase-array antennas such as Phocus Array [16] have been manufactured and its 40 antenna elements operating in the 60 GHz range can be easily fit on a 5 cm × 5 cm board. We assume bandwidth can reach 10 Gbps within the entire data center. Of course, mirror material impacts the performance of wireless link. Reference [15] has tested many reflector materials. Both the cheap, lightweight steel plate and the mirror-quality stainless plate offer perfect reflection. What is more, other reflectors such as standard smooth concrete and plaster walls can also provide not bad even good reflection. This shows our architecture is cheaper and cost less. In short, the system architecture is designed to be feasible.

In order to make sure data transmission can be completed fast and accurately. More details need to be considered carefully. First, when the data transmission is intra-rack, the topology of servers in one rack has been defined, and the distance of two reachable servers is short (less than 3 m), and wireless link is set up easily and reliably. If a wireless link takes place between different racks, the source server has to know the place of the rack where the destination server is positioned, and adjust its antenna to send the wireless signal out. The server relaying the data should know where the data is from and adjust its antenna to receive accurately. So handshake protocol is required to make sure data transmission finished successfully. 20 servers on the top storey is alternative. If there is an idle server for relaying, it should be in the queue and ready to transmit the data. If all of the servers in the destination are busy, the one whose workload is relative light is chose to connect with. In order to reach the goal, three times handshake protocol is designed. The handshake protocol contains three phase. First, the source server sends a data transmission request to the destination server, and then restores the initial state. Second, if the destination server is busy, it transforms the request to other servers on the same storey in clockwise. Then, the idle or not much busy server is chose to reply the request. Finally, the source server sends the confirm message and is ready to set up a wireless link to send data. After the transmission, both servers restore the initial state.

However, adjusting the directional antenna is a very expertise work for the source and destination server. For the source server, it needs to know the location of destination server. So each server positioned on the top storey should contain a global position table, which includes the parameters of all servers on the top storey. If the source server wants to set up a wireless link with others, it makes adjustment according to the details of positions in the table. Of course, if the data center makes some adjustments e.g. a new added server, the global position table should be updated as well. As showed in Fig. 2, if a server s_1 wants to transmit data to a server s_2, it first checks the global position table to find the related parameters about s_2, and makes adjustment to send the data transmission request. If s_2 is idle, it replies the request in the similar way. Then s_1 sends the message to s_2, and is ready to set up the wireless link. Related hand shake algorithm has been listed in Algorithm 2.

Until now, we have known the whole process of setting up an intra- and inter-rack wireless link. This is a recursion procedure. Algorithms about finding shortest path in a graph can be utilized in a data center. Additionally, the whole data center can be viewed as a graph, in which each server is a vertex and its one hop neighbor is another vertex in an edge. So the source server can get a server list to the destination server. Each server in the list tries to send the data to its successor until the destination. Related algorithm is described as Algorithm 3.

Algorithm 2. Handshake(server s_1, server s_2)

Require: s_1 and r_1 is the source server and its rack. s_2 and r_2 is the destination server and its rack.

1: **for** each server s' on the top storey in r_1 **do**
2:     $result\_list_1 \leftarrow$ Intra_Rack_Connection(s_1, s');
3: **end for**
4: **for** each server s' on the top storey in r_2 **do**
5:     $result\_list_2 \leftarrow$ Intra_Rack_Connection(s', s_2);
6: **end for**
7: $result\_list \leftarrow result\_list_1 + result\_list_2$;
8: confirm the state of server the server list $result\_list$;

Algorithm 3. Routing(server s_1, server s_2)

Require: s_1 and r_1 is the source server and its rack. s_2 and r_2 is the destination server and its rack.

1: **if** $r_1 == r_2$ **then**
2:     Intra_Rack_Connection(s_1, s_2)
3: **else**
4:     $server\_list \leftarrow$ Handshake(s_1, s_2)
5:     Transmit data along the $server\_list$.
6: **end if**

---

4   Simulation

Bandwidth is one of the most important performance indicators for a data center. We evaluate the bandwidth of the novel completely wireless data center by counting the number of hops, i.e. if a server can set up a wireless link with its neighbor, the data transmission can be completed by one hop. The less hops of a wireless link, the better bandwidth is. Figure 3 illustrates the performance of bandwidth for our design and Cayley data center when a data center contains 4×4, 6×6, 8×8, and 10×10 racks. It is obvious that bandwidth in our novel design outperforms than Cayley data center. The advantage becomes much more with the scale of data center larger. Our novel wireless data center has good expansibility due to the near constant average number of hops for an data transmission.

Fault tolerance is an another important indicator for a data center. The fault tolerance contains three situations which includes the layer of rack, storey, and server. For the rack layer, as showed in Fig. 4, our novel wireless data center significantly has better performance of fault tolerance than Cayley. The reason is that the inter-rack data transmission, reflecting data to the ceiling, don't relay other racks. Furthermore, there are no signal interference because of independent wireless links. The routing path in Cayley data center contains too many servers which are dependent and influential to each other.

To be honest, for the storey layer, our design, as illustrated in Fig. 5, has worse performance of fault tolerance than Cayley data center. The design of Cayley data center provides many redundant routing paths for a wireless link.

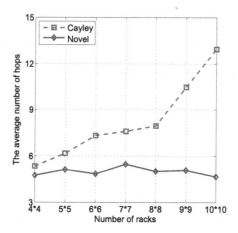

Fig. 3. The number of hops increases with the scale of data center. However, the Cayley data center significantly requires more hops than our novel design.

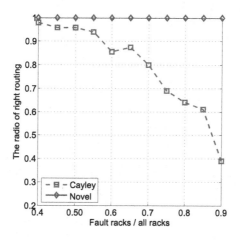

Fig. 4. The fault-tolerance performance of our novel design outperforms than Cayley data center on the rack layer.

When the storey of a rack breaks down, another up or down storey takes place of it. Even though it would make the routing path long, the data transmission can be completed any way. Our novel wireless data center can provide shorter routing path when the fault storey is not large. However, no matter where the source server is positioned, it has to transmit data to the top storey and then to the destination server. It is the source server depending on the servers placed on the upper storeys that brings bad fault-tolerance performance.

However, for the server layer, our novel wireless data center, as showed in Fig. 6, has good performance of fault tolerance and is not worse than Cayley. It is the tradeoff between the inter-communication among racks and the intra-communication among server on a rack.

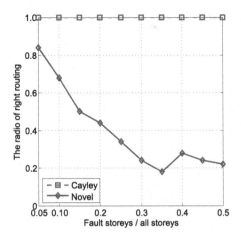

Fig. 5. The fault-tolerance performance in our design is worse than in Cayley data center on the storeys layer.

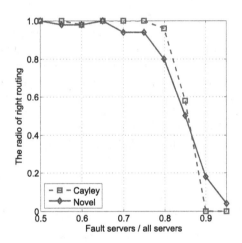

Fig. 6. The fault-tolerance performance in our design is as good as in Cayley data center on the server layer.

Load balance is also essential to the performance of a data center. We evaluate the load balance by counting the number of hotspot emerged in a data center. Hotspot is a server which has much more workload than peers, which always causes the congestion in the data transmission. Besides, too many hotspots in the data center will bring the difficulty of cool service. In the simulation, we randomly generate flows between any two servers. As illustrated in Fig. 7, when a data center has 10×10 racks, it is significant that our novel design has better load-balance performance than Cayley data center. Servers in our novel wireless data center receive less 100 flows. However, more than 10 % servers in Cayley receive more than 100 flows. The most serious server even receives more than

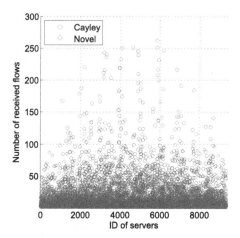

Fig. 7. Our novel design significantly leads to few hotspots than Cayley data center.

300 flows. Our design brings few hotspots because the inter-rack flows reach the destination rack by the reflection, which do not via other racks.

In Cayley wireless data center, each server is installed on two wireless antennas. For a data center, there are hundreds even thousands of servers. It is a big cost will leads to much more energy consumption. Energy consumption is an urgent problem for most of current data centers. For example, the maximum power consumption of a wireless antenna used in Cayley wireless data center is less than 0.3 W. For a 10 × 10 data center (10,000 servers), all servers consume 3 kW, while the same scale of our novel wireless data center only requires 1.5 K.

5   Discussion

Wired data center is commercially mature, and many famous Internet corporations have its data center. However, too complex to deploy and expand, too much power consumption, and too much computing to meet in the era of Big Data exposes its disadvantage. Wireless data center shows its superiority. New 60 GHz transceiver based on standard 90 nm CMOS technology makes it possible to realize. Wireless technology can satisfy requirements and achieve the same level of operation as wires.

60 GHz wireless technology is used in Cayley wireless data center which adopts Cayley graph as the topology of data center network. It has good fault tolerance and can finish data transmission when many racks and servers break down. However, this architecture has two disadvantages at least:

- *Too many routing hops and too much interference.* Good fault tolerance is the advantage of Cayley data center. But this leads too many hops when routing path is set up. The more servers in the routing path, the more load brought in the network and the more interference due to the 60 GHz wireless communication. Our novel wireless data center relizes the inter-rack communication by reflecting the wireless signal to the ceiling. This reduces the workload of other servers and avoids the interference effectively.

- **Cost too much and consume too much energy.** Cost is an important performance for the future prospect of a wireless data center. In Cayley data center, each server utilizes two transceivers. It is a big cost for thousands of servers in a data center. However, a server in our novel data center is installed with only one transceiver. The cost brought by transceivers totally is only about the half of Cayley data center.

Even through our design has many advantages, it also needs some improvements. The future work includes: improving fault tolerance on the level of storey and reducing overload of servers on the top storey.

6   Background and Related Work

Inspired by Cayley graphs, [17] proposes a novel rack design and a multi-hop wireless network for a data center. Servers are placed in prism-shaped containers. Each server utilizes two transceivers for intra- and inter-rack communication. The transceivers are controlled by the Y-switch which is installed in the server. To improve spectrum efficiently, a topology, modeled as a mesh of Cayley graphs, is generalized and a geographic routing protocol is proposed. Our research inherits the design of rack but have designed different routing protocol and communication mechanisms [9], especially for the inter-rack data transmission. Experiments show that the wireless data center, built with our design can potentially, attains higher aggregate bandwidth, lower latency, and substantially higher fault tolerance than the Cayley data center in [17].

However, 60 GHz wireless communication usually has a short range of 10 m and is easy to be blocked by other small obstacles. Inter-rack communication is restricted significantly. Furthermore, inter-rack communication can not always be reliable because of interference caused by other wireless signals. As the scale of data center increases, the interference becomes stronger and will significantly reduce the performance of network. We use highly directional antennas to transmit data and reflect the signals to the ceiling for setting up a wireless link with other racks, which significantly reduce the loss of signal.

7   Conclusion

Traditional wired data centers often suffer from high cost of construction and management and complex wiring. Fortunately, wireless data centers have advantages including economical installing and no worry about wiring. We proposes a novel completely wireless data center, which finishes data transmission by reflecting wireless signal to the ceiling. Especially, the inter-rack data transmission can be finished in average constant hops. Related effective routing protocol has been proposed as well. The extensive simulations evaluate that our novel design of wireless data center performs better than Cayley data center on bandwidth, fault tolerance and effectively decreases the number of hotspot in a data center.

Acknowledgment. The work is supported in part by the National Natural Science Foundation of China (NSFC) under Grant 61402494, Grant 61202487.

References

1. Guo, D., Chen, T., Li, D., Li, M., Liu, Y., Chen, G.: Expandable and cost-effective network structures for data centers using dual-port servers. IEEE Trans. Comput. **62**(7), 1303–1317 (2013)
2. Guo, D., Chen, H., He, Y., Jin, H., Chen, C., Chen, H., Shu, Z., Huang, G.: KCube: a novel architecture for interconnection networks. Elsevier Inf. Process. Lett. **110**(18–19), 821–825 (2010)
3. Guo, D., Zhu, G., Yang, P., Jin, H., Chen, Y., Qi, X., Liu, J.: The product graphs of mobius cube and debruijn digraph. Elsevier Inf. Process. Lett. **112**(5), 205–211 (2012)
4. Al-Fares, M., Loukissas, A., Vahdat, A.: A scalable, commodity data center network architecture. ACM SIGCOMM Comput. Commun. Rev. **38**(4), 63–74 (2008)
5. Niranjan Mysore, R., Pamboris, A., Farrington, N., Huang, N., Miri, P., Radhakrishnan, S., Subramanya, V., Vahdat, A.: Portland: a scalable fault-tolerant layer 2 data center network fabric. ACM SIGCOMM Comput. Commun. Rev. **39**, 39–50 (2009)
6. Greenberg, A., Hamilton, J.R., Jain, N., Kandula, S., Kim, C., Lahiri, P.: VL2: a scalable and flexible data center network. ACM SIGCOMM Comput. Commun. Rev. **39**(4), 51–62 (2009)
7. Farrington, N., Porter, G., Radhakrishnan, S., Bazzaz, H.H., Subramanya, V., Fainman, Y., Papen, G., Vahdat, A.: Helios: a hybrid electrical/optical switch architecture for modular data centers. ACM SIGCOMM Comput. Commun. Rev. **41**(4), 339–350 (2011)
8. Wang, G., Andersen, D.G., Kaminsky, M., Papagiannaki, K., Ng, T., Kozuch, M., Ryan, M.: c-through: part-time optics in data centers. ACM SIGCOMM Comput. Commun. Rev. **40**(4), 327–338 (2010)
9. Halperin, D., Kandula, S., Padhye, J., Bahl, P., Wetherall, D.: Augmenting data center networks with multi-gigabit wireless links. ACM SIGCOMM Comput. Commun. Rev. **41**(4), 38–49 (2011)
10. Williamson, M., Athanasiadou, G., Nix, A.: Investigating the effects of antenna directivity on wireless indoor communication at 60 GHz. In: IEEE International Symposium Personal, Indoor Mobile Radio Communication, vol. 2, pp. 635–639 (1997)
11. Pinel, S., Sen, P., Sarkar, S., Perumana, B., Dawn, D., Yeh, D., Barale, F., Leung, M., Juntunen, E., Vadivelu, P.: 60 GHz single-chip CMOS digital radios and phased array solutions for gaming and connectivity. IEEE J. Sel. Areas Commun. **27**(8), 1347–1357 (2009)
12. Vardhan, H., Thomas, N., Ryu, S.-R., Banerjee, B., Prakash, R.: Wireless data center with millimeter wave network. In: IEEE Global Telecommunications Conference, pp. 1–6 (2010)

13. Ong, E.H., Kneckt, J., Alanen, O., Chang, Z., Huovinen, T., Nihtila, T.: IEEE 802.11 ac: enhancements for very high throughput wlans. In: IEEE International Symposium on Personal, Indoor and Mobile Radio Communications, pp. 849–853 (2011)

14. Smulders, P., Correia, L.: Characterisation of propagation in 60 GHz radio channels. Electron. Commun. Eng. J. 9(2), 73–80 (1997)

15. Zhou, X., Zhang, Z., Zhu, Y., Li, Y., Kumar, S., Vahdat, A., Zhao, B.Y., Zheng, H.: Mirror mirror on the ceiling: flexible wireless links for data centers. ACM SIGCOMM Comput. Commun. Rev. 42(4), 443–454 (2012)

16. Phocus array system. http://www.fidelity-comtech.com/products/phocus-array/

17. Shin, J.-Y., Sirer, E.G., Weatherspoon, H., Kirovski, D.: On the feasibility of completely wireless datacenters. In: ACM/IEEE Architectures for Networking and Communications Systems, pp. 3–14 (2012)

A Personalized k-Anonymity with Fake Position Generation for Location Privacy Protection

Zhi Luo and Xiaohong Huang$^{(\boxtimes)}$

Institute of Network Technology,
Beijing University of Posts and Telecommunications, Beijing, China
luozhil989@gmail.com, huangxh@bupt.edu.cn

Abstract. Privacy protection has become one of the important issues for location-based services (LBS) nowadays. In order to meet the requirements of humanization, security and quick response, this paper proposes an improved personalized k-anonymous location privacy protection algorithm with fake position generation mechanism. Compared to the normal personalized k-anonymity algorithm, our improved algorithm has higher success rate of anonymity. By generating fake queries for the source queries that expire, our algorithm guarantees that no source query will be dropped, namely all the source queries can get anonymized. The experimental results show that the algorithm proposed by this paper is able to achieve better performance in terms of success rate of anonymity.

Keywords: k-anonymity · Privacy · Location-based services

1 Introduction

In the past few years, more and more location-detection devices, such as cellular phones, GPS-like devices and RFID are widely used, which results in a surge of location based services, including Foursquare [1], Google Latitude [2] and Where [3]. People's lives become more convenient with the increasing number of LBS, but unfortunately, LBS may threaten the users' privacy.

When a user use his mobile client to requests a LBS, for example, to get the information about how many restaurants nearby from an LBS provider, the user must submit his service query with raw position information. So the LBS provider can collect the information about where the user is, what the user want to do and even who is the user! Assuming that this LBS provider are not trusted but semi honest, these raw position information may be leaked to other people and thus the user's location privacy is leaked.

The major privacy threat specific to LBS usage is the location privacy breaches represented by space or time correlated inference attacks [4], to eliminate this threat, efficient ways need to be found. There is a rich collection of literature that aims at protecting user's location privacy, which mainly can be divided into three categories [5]:

- Pseudonym, for any LBS request, users use a trusted middleware (such as hash functions, etc.) to generate an alternative user identification information to protect their privacy [6, 7];

S. Zhang et al. (Eds.): ICoC 2014, CCIS 502, pp. 46–55, 2015.
DOI: 10.1007/978-3-662-46826-5_4

- Method based on privacy information retrieval (Privacy Information Retrieval, PIR) [8, 9], which protects users' privacy by encrypting location data. This method utilizes cryptographic protocols such as homomorphic encryption, so it has great strength of protection without excessive exposure of location information stored in the database of LBS servers. But the communication costs and computing costs of the method are very high.
- Anonymous method based on location, which uses the region (containing the user's position) query instead of the point query.

One of the most popular location privacy techniques is k-anonymity approach, which consists in cloaking users' locations such that k users appear as potential senders of a query, thus achieving k-anonymity. In this paper, after the analysis of the efficiency of normal personalized k-anonymity algorithm [4] and its drawbacks, we came up with an improved personalized k-anonymity in protecting location privacy which is more efficient and more reasonable than the normal one.

The rest of paper is organized as follows: in Sect. 2, we introduce the related work in the study of k-anonymity approach. In Sect. 3, we present our improved personalized k-anonymity algorithms. In Sect. 4, we present the simulation results of our improved algorithm and the normal personalized k-anonymity algorithm. Finally we summarize our contributions and discuss directions for future work.

2 Related Work

The concept of location k-anonymity is originally introduced in the context of relational data privacy [10], which aims to address the question of "how a data holder can release its private data with guarantees that the individual subjects of the data cannot be identified whereas the data remain practically useful" [11]. This concept is firstly introduced in [12] as a natural extension of the k-anonymity model for relational data records, it deals with the anonymous release of real-time location data to LBSs with certain anonymity guarantees.

The traditional k-anonymity approach in protecting location privacy uses a quadtree data structure built in the anonymity server to divide the entire area into minimum constraint rectangles (MBR) recursively, each MBR corresponds to a user node. This approach assumes that all the queries (say q) from users have a unified anonymity level represented by an integer value (say q.k), this mechanism does not meet the user's individual privacy requirements obviously. Furthermore, anonymous region is determined by the maximum of q.k, if there is a query with larger q.k, the entire region of anonymity may be very large. In this case, the degree of protection was not significantly improved for some queries with low privacy requirements, instead, the quality of service (QoS) decreases and the communication cost increases.

Buğra Gedik and Ling Liu came up with an approach that uses spatio-temporal cloaking to transform each original query from a mobile node into a privacy protected query with the k-anonymity guarantee [4]. In their approach, in order to meet different location privacy requirements of users and ensure varying levels of LBS quality, each user specifies its own anonymity level (k value), spatial tolerance and temporal tolerance. Each query of users is sent to a location anonymity server, whose main task is to transform the query into a new query that can be safely (k-anonymity) sent to the LBS provider. The key idea that underlies the location k-anonymity is twofold. First, regardless of population density, a given degree of location anonymity can be maintained by decreasing the location accuracy through enlarging the exposed spatial area so that there are other $k - 1$ queries present in the same spatial area, this approach is called spatial cloaking. Second, location anonymity can be achieved by delaying the query until k queries have visited the same area, this approach is called temporal cloaking.

Buğra Gedik and Ling Liu's approach meets user's individual privacy requirements and achieves personalized k-anonymity to a certain degree, but still has following problems:

- When searching for a clique for a query q in the constraint graph, it only ensures that q should be included in the clique with size of q.k, but in fact the clique with bigger size may exists so that more queries can be anonymized at one time.
- Every query in an available clique with size of k must has at least $k - 1$ other queries in this clique as its neighbors, this requirement is unnecessary and it reduces the chance to find an available clique.
- Each query has its own survival period and a deadline, when a query is beyond its deadline, it has to be dropped. This mechanism undoubtedly reduces the quality of service because the user whose query is dropped cannot get any desired responses. One solution to this problem is to generate fake queries for the source queries that expire. He Kang has proposed a solution, which is that the anonymity server randomly generates some fake queries in the whole constraint graph at a fixed time every day [13]. This solution cannot guarantee every query can get anonymized because the fake queries are randomly generated, and resources are wasted due to some fake queries may never be used.

In this paper, based on the normal personalized k-anonymity algorithm proposed by Buğra Gedik and Ling Liu, we propose an improved personalized k-anonymity algorithm with fake position generation mechanism in protecting location privacy so that the three questions mentioned above can be addressed efficiently.

3 Proposed Personalized k-Anonymity Algorithm

3.1 Notations

For reference convenience, we summarize the important notations below, which will be used throughout the rest of the paper (See Table 1).

3.2 Data Structures

The following four data structures will be used in the anonymity algorithm [4].

- Q_q, a simple first-in, first-out (FIFO) queue that collects the queries ordered by the time they are received from the users.

Table 1.

S	Source query set
T	Transformed query set
q_s	A query in set S
q_t	A query in set T
$R(q_s)$	Transformed format of q_s
k	Anonymity level
d_x, d_y, d_t	spatial and temporal tolerances
$C(q_s) = (x, y)$	Spatial point of q_s
$L(q_s) = (x, y, t)$	Spatial-temporal point of q_s
$A_{cn}(q_s)$	Spatial constraint box of q_s
$A_{cl}(q_t)$	Spatial constraint box of q_t
$B_{cn}(q_s)$	Spatio-temporal constraint box of q_s
$B_{cl}(q_t)$	Spatio-temporal cloaking box of q_t
MBR	Minimum bounding rectangle, namely the smallest rectangle that contains all the points
$B_q(S')$	MBR of a set of source queries
$G_q(S, E)$	Constraint graph
$Nbr(q_s, G_q)$	Neighbors of q_s in G_q

- I_q, a multidimensional index that allows efficient search on the spatio-temporal points of the queries. I_q contains a 3D point $L(q_s)$ as a key, together with the query q_s as data. The index is implemented by R*-tree [14].
- G_q, a dynamic graph, which contains the queries that are not yet anonymized and not yet dropped due to expiration.
- H_q, a mean heap sorted based on the deadline of the queries.

In order to solve the problems of the normal algorithm proposed by Buğra Gedik and Ling Liu which are mentioned in Sect. 2, we added three new data structures that will be used in our improved algorithm:

- I_q', instead of I_q that mentioned above, we use a two-dimensional index I_q' that only allows search on the spatial points of the queries. I_q' contains a 2D point $C(q_s)$ as a key, together with the query q_s as data.
- T_A, a two-dimensional interval tree to hold rectangular regions, which allows efficient retrieval of all points in the corresponding rectangular region [15]. In our algorithm, we build T_A based on the $A_{cn}(q_s)$.

N_t, the tree node of T_A. Each N_t contains an integer value s which represents the number of regions that overlap the region held by N_t. Each leaf node of T_A holds a unit rectangle, which in fact is a square with side length of 1.

3.3   Algorithms

Algorithm 1. improved k-anonymity algorithm.
1.   while server_running = true
2.   if Q_q != $\varnothing$
3. q_{sc} ← Pop the first item in Q_q
4.   Put q_{sc} into I_q' with $C(q_{sc})$
5.   Put q_{sc} into H_q with $(q_{sc}.t + q_{sc}.d_t)$
6.   Put q_{sc} into G_q as a node
7. G_q' ← GET_SUBGRAPH(q_{sc})
8.   Q ← LOCAL-k_SEARCH(q_{sc}, G_q')
9.   OUTPUT(Q)
10.   while true
11. q_s ← Topmost item in H_q
12.   if $q_s.t + q_s.d_t$ < time point of now
13. G_q' ← GET_SUBGRAPH(q_s)
14.   Q ← GENERATE_QUERIES(q_s, G_q')
15.   OUTPUT(Q)
16.   else
17.   break

Algorithm 2. GET_SUBGRAPH(q_{sc})
1.   N ← Range search I_q' using $A_{cn}(q_{sc})$
2.   foreach q_s ∈ N, q_s != q_{sc}
3.   if $C(q_{sc})$ ∈ $A_{cn}(q_s)$
4.   Add edge (q_{sc}, q_s) into G_q
5. G_q' ← Subgraph of G_q consisting of queries in N
6.   return G_q'

Algorithm 3. improved local-k_search algorithm
  LOCAL-k_SEARCH(q_{sc}, G_q')
1.   if $|nbr(q_{sc}, G_q') + 1|$ < $q_{sc}.k$
2.   return $\varnothing$
3.   U ← {q_s | q_s ∈ $nbr(q_{sc}, G_q')$ and $q_s.k$ <= $|nbr(q_{sc}, G_q') + 1|$}
4.   if $|U|$ < $q_{sc}.k - 1$
5.   return $\varnothing$
6.   1 ← 0
7.   while 1 != $|U|$
8.   1 ← $|U|$
9.   foreach q_s ∈ U
10.   if ($q_s.k$ > $|U| + 1$ or $|nbr(q_s, G_q') ∩ U|$ < $q_s.k - 2$)
11.   U ← U \ {q_s}
12.   Find any subset Q of U, s.t.
13. $|Q|$ >= k − 1 and Q ∪ {q_{sc}} forms a clique
14.   if Q found
15.   return Q ∪ {q_{sc}}
16.   else
17.   return $\varnothing$

Algorithm 4. OUTPUT(Q)
1.   If $Q \mathrel{!}= \varnothing$
2.   Randomize the order of queries in Q
3.   foreach q_s in Q
4.   Output anonymized queries
5. $q_t \leftarrow \{q_s.u_{id}, q_s.q_{no}, A_q(Q), q_s.C\}$
6.   Remove the query q_s from G_q, I_q', H_q

Algorithm 5. GENERATE_QUERIES(q_{sc}, G_q')
1. $T_A \leftarrow$ Build a T_A based on region $A_{cn}(q_{sc})$
2. $L \leftarrow \varnothing$
3.   foreach leaf node N_t in T_a
4. $N_t.s \leftarrow 1$
5. $L \leftarrow L \cup \{N_t\}$
6. $U \leftarrow \{q_s \mid q_s \in nbr(q_{sc}, G_q')$ and $q_s.k <= q_{sc}.k \}$
7.   foreach $q_s \in U$
8. $R \leftarrow \{r \mid r$ is a unit rectangle and r is a sub region of $A_{cn}(q_s)\}$
9.   foreach $r \in R$
10.   Binary search r in T_A, if there exists a $N_t \in L$ that holds r
11. $N_t.s \leftarrow N_t.s + 1$
12. $F \leftarrow \varnothing$
13. while $|U| + |F| < q_{sc}.k - 1$
14.   foreach $N_t \in L$ in decreasing order of $N_t.s$
15. $q_f \leftarrow$ Generate a fake query in the region held by N_t
16.   Add edge (q_f, q_{sc}) into G_q'
17. $F \leftarrow F \cup \{q_f\}$
18.   if $|U| + |F| == q_{sc}.k - 1$
19.   break
20. foreach $q_s \in U$
21.   while $|nbr(q_s, G_q'')| < q_s.k - 2$
22.   foreach $N_t \in L$ holds $A_{cn}(q_s)$'s sub region in decreasing order of $N_t.s$
23. $q_f \leftarrow$ Generate a fake query in the region held by N_t
24.   Add edge (q_f, q_s) into G_q'
25. $F \leftarrow F \cup \{q_f\}$
26. $|nbr(q_s, G_q')| == q_s.k - 2$
27.   break
28. return $U \cup F \cup \{q_{sc}\}$

Algorithm 1 describes the entire process of our improved anonymity algorithm, which is similar to the normal personalized k-anonymity algorithm [4]. The rest of this section we will tell the differences between our algorithm and the normal one, and also explain why our algorithm is better and how it works.

We use I_q' instead of I_q because more queries can be included without the constraint of time. For convenience, we extract the steps 7–11 and the steps 13–18 from the normal personalized k-anonymity algorithm [4] to create Algorithm 2 and Algorithm 4 respectively. So, Algorithm 2 is responsible for generating sub-graph G_q' from G_q, which consisting all the neighbor queries of q_{sc} in the range of $A_{cn}(q_{sc})$. Algorithm 4 is responsible for anonymizing every query in a available clique which is found in Algorithm 3 or Algorithm 5.

In Algorithm 3, improved local-k_search algorithm, step 3, we collect q_s in nbr(q_{sc}, G_q') with $q_s.k \leq |nbr(q_{sc}, G_q') + 1|$ instead of $q_s.k \leq q_{sc}.k$ in normal local-k_search algorithm [4] because $|nbr(q_{sc}, G_q') + 1|$ is no less than $q_{sc}.k$ ($\emptyset$ is returned before this step if $|nbr(q_{sc}, G_q') + 1| < q_{sc}.k$), so that we may find more queries to form a clique with a bigger size. The clique with a bigger size undoubtedly provides better privacy protection against linking attacks, and it also makes every q_s have more chances to get anonymized without generating fake queries. In step 10, instead of $|nbr(q_s, G_q')| \cap U| < k - 2$ in normal local-k_search algorithm [4], we use ($q_s.k > |U| + 1$ or $|nbr(q_s, G_q')| \cap U| < q_s.k - 2$) to judge whether q_s can exists in U, which is more likely to find an available clique for q_{sc}.

In Algorithm 1, improved k-anonymity algorithm, when an expired query is checked, we use Algorithm 5 to generate fake queries for it to form a clique other than simply drop it.

A fake query, say q_f, is considered with no spatio-temporal constraint box, so it can be a neighbor of each true source query q_s as long as $C(q_f)$ is in the $A_{cn}-(q_s)$. We also consider that q_f does not need anonymity, namely $q_f.k = 1$.

Generating a q_f in a region overlapped by more $A_{cn}-(q_s)$ is more likely to get more q_s which don't have enough neighbors to have one more fake neighbor at one time, thus the whole generating process may take less time as well as less fake queries. The basis of this idea is the reason why we count the $N_t.s$ of each N_t in T_A. By $N_t.s$, we put all the N_t in T_A in decreasing order and by this order, we generate one q_f in the region held by the corresponding N_t at one time, and do this process cyclically until no more fake queries are needed. This mechanism also avoids that fake queries are only concentrated in some regions held by the N_t with larger $N_t.s$.

4   Experiments and Results

Success rate of anonymity is an important measure for evaluating the effectiveness of the proposed location k-anonymity algorithm [4]. In this section, we compare our improved algorithm's success rate of anonymity with the success rate of anonymity of Buğra Gedik and Ling Liu's normal algorithm in different cases.

We use a two-dimensional coordinates of 100×100 as the dynamic graph G which mentioned in the section above, and generate source queries q_s whose $C(q_s)$ is the integer coordinate points in the G randomly.

Figure 1 shows the success rate of anonymity for the normal algorithm and our improved algorithm. The success rate is shown (on the y-axis) for different groups of queries, each group representing the number of source queries (on the x-axis). Every source query q_s with its $q_s.k$ ranges from 2 to 5.

As we can see from the Fig. 1, with the increasing number of source queries, the average success rate of both algorithms are also increasing. The success rate of our improved algorithm is always higher than the normal one's and the less source queries are, the advantage of our improved algorithm are more obvious.

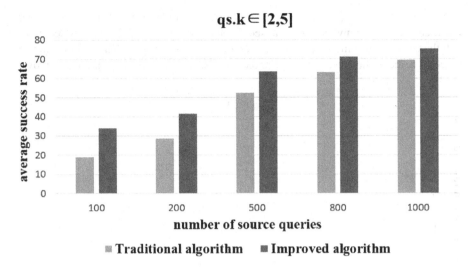

Fig. 1. Success rates for different number of source queries.

Figure 2 shows the success rate of anonymity for the normal algorithm and our improved algorithm with 1000 source queries respectively. Each number on the x-axis, represents the maximum number (say MAX) of $q_s.k$ for all queries in the corresponding group, which means that each $q_s.k$ in its group ranges from 2 to MAX. The average success rate of anonymity is shown (on the y-axis) for different groups of MAX of $q_s.k$.

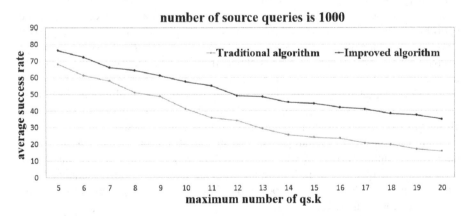

Fig. 2. Number of anonymized queries with respect to different maximum numbers of $q_s.k$.

From Fig. 2, we can see that with the increase of maximum number of $q_s.k$, the average success rate of anonymity decreases for both algorithms, but our improved algorithm has better performance compared to the performance of the normal algorithm. The success rate represented by our improved algorithm is always higher than the one represented by the normal algorithm.

Figure 3 shows the percentage of fake queries generated over the different number of source queries, from which, we can see that the percentage of fake queries decreases with the increasing number of the source queries. This is because that the more source queries are, the higher success rate of anonymity is, which is shown in the Fig 1 above.

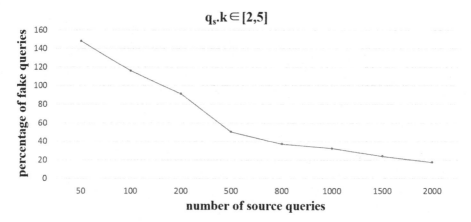

Fig. 3. Percentage of fake queries generated over the number of source queries.

5   Conclusion

In this paper, we have presented an improved personalized k-anonymity algorithm in protecting location privacy. Compared with the normal personalized k-anonymity algorithm proposed by Buğra Gedik and Ling Liu, our algorithm may find a clique with bigger size for each query from users. We can also guarantee that every query can get anonymized by generating fake queries efficiently for the queries which expire, so that the no query will be dropped due to expiration.

We have conducted the experiment for our improved algorithm and the normal personalized k-anonymity algorithm. The results show that our algorithm has obvious advantages over the normal one in terms of success rate of anonymity.

With fake position generation mechanism, our approach guarantees that every query can get anonymized, but when the $A_{cn}(q_s)$ is very large, it may take lots of time to generate fake queries for q_s. So, we are studying new ways which including better data structures to hold regions and better algorithm to make the process of generating fake queries more efficient.

Acknowledgement. The paper is sponsored by Beijing Higher Education Young Elite Teacher Project, DNSLAB, the China's Next Generation Internet Project(CNGI Project)(CNGI-12-03-009) and National High Technology Research and Development Program of China (2013AA014702).

Reference

1. Foursquare. https://foursquare.com/. Accessed April 2014
2. Google Latitude. https://www.google.com/latitude/. Accessed April 2014
3. Where, http://where.com. Accessed April 2014
4. Gedik, B., Liu, L.: Protecting location privacy with personalized k-anonymity: architecture and algorithms, IEEE Trans. Mob. Comput. **7**(1), 1–18, (2008)
5. Xiao, P., Zhen, X., Xiaofeng, M.: Survey of location privacy preserving. J. Comput. Sci. Front. **1**(3), 268–281 (2007)
6. Xiao, Z., Meng, X., Xu, J.: Quality Aware Privacy Protection for Location—Based Services, pp. 434–446. Springer, Heidelberg (2007)
7. Kido, H., Yanagisawa, Y., Satoh, T.: An anonymous communication technique using dummies for location based services. In: IEEE International Conference on Pervasive Services, pp. 88–97 (2005)
8. Jang, M.Y., Jang, S.J., Chang, J.W.: A New KNN query processing algorithm enhancing privacy protection in location based services. In: IEEE First International Conference on Mobile Services, pp. 17–24 (2012)
9. Kalnis, P., Ghinita, G., Mouratidis, K., et al.: Preventing location based identify inference in anonymous spatial queries. IEEE Trans. Knowl. Data Eng. **19**(12), 1719–1733 (2007)
10. Samarati, P., Sweeney L.: Protecting privacy when disclosing information: k-anonymity and its enforcement through generalization and suppression. In: Proceedings of IEEE Symposium on Research in Security and Privacy (1998)
11. Sweeney, L.: k-anonymity: a model for protecting privacy. IJUFKS, **10**(5), 557–570 (2002)
12. Gruteser, M., Grunwald, D.: Anonymous usage of location based services through spatial and temporal cloaking. In: ACM/USENIX MobiSys (2003)
13. Kang, H.: The research and implementation of personalized k-anonymous location privacy protection technology based on the internet of things. J. Nanjing Univ. Posts Telecommun. (Natural Science Edition) TP393.08, **28**(6), 78–82 (2012)
14. Beckmann, N., Kriegel, H.-P., Schneider, R., Seeger, B.: R±Tree: an efficient and robust access method for points and rectangles. In: Proceeding of ACM International Conference Management of Data (Sigmod 1990), pp. 322–331 (1990)
15. Interval Tree. http://en.wikipedia.org/wiki/Interval_tree. Accessed April 2014.

A Localization Algorithm
for Wireless Sensor Networks

Zhi Li[1,2(✉)], Yingyou Wen[1,2], Yinghui Meng[1,2], and Hong Zhao[1]

[1] School of Information Science and Engineering,
Northeastern University, Shenyang, China
remcall@163.com
[2] Key Laboratory of Medical Image Computing,
Northeastern University, Shenyang, China

Abstract. Node localization is important in many WSN applications. Most of existing algorithms are not applicable for networks in a concave area. To address this problem, a novel localization algorithm is proposed. The key of this algorithm is the design of neighborhood function which only uses distances between neighbor nodes to generate a new set of estimated locations from an old set. Both range-based and range-free localization can use it to estimate locations of nodes if distances between neighbor nodes are measured by hardware or estimated by distance estimation algorithms. Simulation results indicate that this algorithm can achieve accurate and reliable localization results in a concave area.

Keywords: Localization · Concave area · Neighborhood function · Wireless sensor network

1 Introduction

Wireless sensor network (WSN) is composed of many battery-powered and low-cost sensor nodes which are used to sense data from the environment (e.g., light, humidity, temperature, etc.) [1]. Sensor data gathered by nodes are insignificant unless we know where the data are obtained from, and sensor data with their own clear locations can detail where the specific event happens. Besides, locations of nodes are also needed for many applications, like geographic routing, network topology based on geometric techniques and energy conservation [2–5].

However, nodes are often randomly deployed in inaccessible regions and locations of nodes are always uncontrollable. Although nodes can obtain their accurate locations by configuring Global Positioning System (GPS) adapters or manual configuration, the two methods are not suitable for wireless sensor networks considering expensive cost or specific limitation in some environments [6]. Hence, node localization is an important and challenging topic in wireless sensor networks.

In area-based algorithms, a non-anchor's location is estimated by picking up a point within an area formed by anchors, like Centroid [7, 8] and APIT [9]. Centroid estimates a non-anchor's location as the centroid of the polygon formed by anchors that are within the communication range of the non-anchor. APIT uses the redundancy of available anchors and pinpoints a non-anchor's location to the intersection of all

© Springer-Verlag Berlin Heidelberg 2015
S. Zhang et al. (Eds.): ICoC 2014, CCIS 502, pp. 56–67, 2015.
DOI: 10.1007/978-3-662-46826-5_5

containing triangles which contain the non-anchor. Distance-based algorithms calculate non-anchors' locations through distances between nodes.

Distance-based algorithms involve two steps: (1) distances between neighbor nodes are measured by hardware or estimated by distance estimation algorithms. (2) non-anchors' locations are estimated by localization algorithms based on distances obtained from the first step.

According to different methods of distances calculating, distance-based algorithms can be further divided into two categories: range-based and range-free. Range-based algorithms, such as the time of arrival (TOA) [10], time difference of arrival (TDOA) [11, 12], angle of arrival (AOA) [13] and received signal strength (RSS) [14], calculate distances between neighbor nodes by some typical hardware. By contrast, range-free algorithms, such as DV-Hop [15], DV-RND [16], RSD [17] and LEAP [18], design some distance estimation algorithms to calculate distances between nodes by the communication and connectivity. They do not need specific hardware support. After distances between neighbor nodes are calculated, the shortest distances between any pair of nodes can be inferred by the lengths of the shortest paths. Note that two nodes are neighbor nodes if they can communicate with each other directly.

Then, localization algorithms, like Multilateration [19] and MDS-MAP [20], are performed to estimate non-anchors' locations. Multilateration uses the shortest distances between a non-anchor and more than three anchors to calculate the non-anchor's location. MDS-MAP estimates non-anchors' locations by using the shortest distances between any pair of nodes. We can see both Multilateration and MDS-MAP use the shortest distances between nodes. Such algorithms are achievable only when the shortest paths are close to straight lines (i.e., the shortest distances between nodes are almost equal to the Euclidean distances), which requires that nodes are uniformly and densely distributed in a convex area.

However, when nodes are deployed in a concave area, the shortest paths between some nodes have to detour along the concave area and cannot be close to a straight line no matter how densely nodes are deployed. To address this problem, this paper proposes a novel greedy optimization localization algorithm (GOLA) with two correction operations for WSNs in a concave area.

2   Related Work

Multilateration [19] is applicable when distances between a non-anchor and more than three anchors are known or calculated. It uses the least squares fitting algorithm to estimate the non-anchor's location, and it is based on the belief that all distances are close to the Euclidean distances. However, when the non-anchor and anchors are not neighbor nodes, the shortest distances between them may deviate far away from their Euclidean distances in a concave area and lead to high localization error.

The paper [21] improves Multilateration by using four nearest anchors instead of using all anchors, but it is still possible that the shortest distances to the nearest four anchors are affected by concave shapes.

The paper [22] proposes a PDM (proximity-distance map) algorithm. PDM assumes that there exists a linear function between the shortest distances and the Euclidean distances of all pairs of anchors. However, it is not easy to find such a linear function when nodes are randomly deployed.

MDS-MAP [20] uses multidimensional scaling to estimate non-anchors' locations. MDS-MAP first constructs a matrix which contains the shortest distances between any pair of nodes. Then, MDS-MAP applies classical MDS to the matrix and retains the first d eigenvectors to construct a d-dimensional relative map. Finally, MDS-MAP transforms the relative map to an absolute map based on the absolute locations of anchors. We can see MDS-MAP also uses the shortest distances which lead to high localization error in a concave area.

To address this problem, the paper [23] proposes CMDS (cluster-based MDS) algorithm. CMDS forms a number of k-hop clusters for localization and performs MDS-MAP for each cluster. Then CMDS gets its own coordinate system by merging coordinate system of all clusters. However, CMDS requires hierarchical network architecture, and it is difficult to determine the value of k-hop.

3 Greedy Optimization Localization Algorithm

3.1 Neighborhood Function

(1) Network Model
In this paper, we focus on the second step of distance-based algorithm (i.e., distances between neighbor nodes can be measured by typical hardware in range-based algorithms or calculated by some distance estimation algorithms in range-free algorithms).

i and j are non-anchors nodes. k is an anchor. j and k are neighbor nodes of i. da_{ik} and ds_{ij} are the distances between neighbor nodes. Because no matter how to get the distances, da_{ik} and ds_{ij} have distance errors. Hence, we model da_{ik} and ds_{ij} as follows:

$$da_{ik} = d_{ik} + e_{ik} = d_{ik} * (1 + \alpha * randn(1))$$
$$ds_{ij} = d_{ij} + e_{ij} = d_{ij} * (1 + \alpha * randn(1))$$
$$d_{ik} = \sqrt{(x_i - x_k)^2 + (y_i - y_k)^2} \qquad (1)$$
$$d_{ij} = \sqrt{(x_i - x_j)^2 + (y_i - y_j)^2}$$

where d_{ik} and d_{ij} are the Euclidean distances; e_{ik} and e_{ij} are distance errors. We assume these errors follow a zero-mean Gaussian distribution with variance $\sigma^2 = \alpha^2 d^2$. We realize that this assumption does not capture all practical cases, but it is a good starting point for exploring the impact of distance errors on localization algorithms in WSNs. We use (2) to calculate estimated distances $\overline{da}_{ik}$ and $\overline{ds}_{ij}$:

$$\overline{da}_{ik}=\sqrt{\left(\overline{x}_i-x_k\right)^2+\left(\overline{y}_i-y_k\right)^2}$$
$$\overline{ds}_{ij}=\sqrt{\left(\overline{x}_i-\overline{x}_j\right)^2+\left(\overline{y}_i-\overline{y}_j\right)^2} \tag{2}$$

wa_{ik} and ws_{ij} are the correct neighbor relation. The value of wa_{ik} or ws_{ij} is 1 if two nodes are neighbor nodes (i.e., $d_{ik} \leq R$ or $d_{ij} \leq R$), otherwise 0.

(2) Design of Neighborhood Function
According to the description of network model, the localization problem can be formulated as:

$$\min \left(\begin{array}{l} CF = \displaystyle\sum_{i=1}^{n}\sum_{k=1}^{m} wa_{ik} \cdot \left(da_{ik}-\overline{da}_{ik}\right)^2 \\ \quad + \displaystyle\sum_{i=1}^{n}\sum_{j=1}^{n} ws_{ij} \cdot \left(ds_{ij}-\overline{ds}_{ij}\right)^2 \end{array} \right) \tag{3}$$

where CF is the squared error between the estimated distances and real distances of neighbor nodes. Note that da_{ik} and ds_{ij} are considered as the real distances in this paper. Our aim is to find a set of estimated locations of non-anchors to minimize the value of the objective function CF. CF can also represent the quantitative measure of the accuracy of the estimated locations (the smaller CF is, the more accurate estimated locations are).

To optimize CF, we need a neighborhood function which is used to generate a new solution from an old solution (a solution is a set of estimated locations of non-anchors). The design of neighborhood function is depended on the characteristics of the problem and the expression of the solution.

We assume that we obtain a new solution S^{new} through iterative computation and S^{new} is generated from an old solution S^{old}. We assume the estimated coordinates in S^{new} are perfect (note that this assumption is just used to derive neighborhood function). That is, the estimated distances between neighbor nodes are equal to the real distances.

We first consider the estimated distance $\overline{ds}_{ij}^{new}$ between neighbor non-anchors i and j as follows:

$$\left(\overline{ds}_{ij}^{new}\right)^2 = \left(\overline{x}_i^{new} - \overline{x}_j^{new}\right)^2 + \left(\overline{y}_i^{new} - \overline{y}_j^{new}\right)^2 = ds_{ij}^2 \tag{4}$$

Where $(\overline{x}_i^{new},\overline{y}_i^{new})$ and $(\overline{x}_j^{new}, \overline{y}_j^{new})$ are estimated coordinates of non-anchors i and j in S^{new}. In S^{old}, the estimated distance $\overline{ds}_{ij}^{old}$ between neighbor non-anchors i and j can be calculated by:

$$\left(\overline{ds}_{ij}^{old}\right)^2 = \left(\overline{x}_i^{old} - \overline{x}_j^{old}\right)^2 + \left(\overline{y}_i^{old} - \overline{y}_j^{old}\right)^2 \tag{5}$$

Where $(\overline{x}_i^{old}, \overline{y}_i^{old})$ and $(\overline{x}_i^{old}, \overline{y}_i^{old})$ are estimated coordinates of non-anchors i and j in S^{old}. By using (4) and (5), we can get:

$$
\begin{aligned}
\left(\overline{x}_i^{new} - \overline{x}_j^{new}\right)^2 + \left(\overline{y}_i^{new} - \overline{y}_j^{new}\right)^2 &= ds_{ij}^2 \\
&= \left[\frac{ds_{ij}}{\overline{ds}_{ij}^{old}} \cdot \left(\overline{x}_i^{old} - \overline{x}_j^{old}\right)\right]^2 + \left[\frac{ds_{ij}}{\overline{ds}_{ij}^{old}} \cdot \left(\overline{y}_i^{old} - \overline{y}_j^{old}\right)\right]^2
\end{aligned}
\tag{6}
$$

By analyzing (6), we can obtain the relation of the abscissa and ordinate coordinates:

$$
\begin{aligned}
\overline{x}_i^{new} - \overline{x}_j^{new} &= \frac{ds_{ij}}{\overline{ds}_{ij}^{old}} \cdot \left(\overline{x}_i^{old} - \overline{x}_j^{old}\right) \\
\overline{y}_i^{new} - \overline{y}_j^{new} &= \frac{ds_{ij}}{\overline{ds}_{ij}^{old}} \cdot \left(\overline{y}_i^{old} - \overline{y}_j^{old}\right)
\end{aligned}
\tag{7}
$$

We can see that (7) is the sufficient condition of (6). If any non-anchor i ($1 \le i \le n$) meets (7) with all its neighbor nodes including the non-anchors and anchors in S^{new}, we consider that the estimated locations must be correct because the value of CF is 0 and the estimated locations must meet the follow equations:

$$
\begin{aligned}
&\sum_{k=1}^{m} wa_{ik} \cdot \left(\overline{x}_i^{new} - x_k\right) + \sum_{j=1}^{n} ws_{ij} \cdot \left(\overline{x}_i^{new} - \overline{x}_j^{new}\right) \\
&= \sum_{k=1}^{m} wa_{ik} \cdot \frac{da_{ik}}{\overline{da}_{ik}^{old}} \cdot \left(\overline{x}_i^{old} - x_k\right) + \sum_{j=1}^{n} ws_{ij} \cdot \frac{ds_{ij}}{\overline{ds}_{ij}^{old}} \cdot \left(\overline{x}_i^{old} - \overline{x}_j^{old}\right) \\
&\sum_{k=1}^{m} wa_{ik} \cdot \left(\overline{y}_i^{new} - y_k\right) + \sum_{j=1}^{n} ws_{ij} \cdot \left(\overline{y}_i^{new} - \overline{y}_j^{new}\right) \\
&= \sum_{k=1}^{m} wa_{ik} \cdot \frac{da_{ik}}{\overline{da}_{ik}^{old}} \cdot \left(\overline{y}_i^{old} - y_k\right) + \sum_{j=1}^{n} ws_{ij} \cdot \frac{ds_{ij}}{\overline{ds}_{ij}^{old}} \cdot \left(\overline{y}_i^{old} - \overline{y}_j^{old}\right)
\end{aligned}
\tag{8}
$$

Equation (7) is the sufficient condition of (8), but not the necessary and sufficient condition. That is, if the estimated location of any non-anchor i meets (8), it may be correct. Of course, it may not be correct.

However, as $da_{ik}\big/\overline{da}_{ik}^{\,old}$ and $ds_{ij}\big/\overline{ds}_{ij}^{\,old}$ is used to correct the coordinates of the non-anchor i and all its neighbor nodes in S^{old}, S^{new} may be more accurate than S^{old}. Just because of this uncertainty, we use CF to distinguish which solution is more accurate (the smaller CF is, the more accurate the solution is).

If estimated coordinates of all non-anchors meet (8), we use matrices to express the relation:

$$(W1 + W2) \cdot \overline{S}^{new} - WA \cdot A = (D1 + D2) \cdot \overline{S}^{old} - D3 \cdot A \tag{9}$$

Where $WA = [wa_{ik}]_{n \times m}$ denotes the correct neighbor relation matrix between non-anchors and anchors.

Matrices $W_1 = [w1_{ij}]_{n \times n}$, $W2 = [w2_{ij}]_{n \times n}$, $D1 = [d1_{ij}]_{n \times n}$, $D2 = [d2_{ij}]_{n \times n}$ and $D3 = [d3_{ik}]_{n \times m}$ can be calculated as follows:

$$w1_{ij} = \begin{cases} \sum\limits_{j=1}^{n} ws_{ij} & i = j \\ -ws_{ij} & otherwise \end{cases} , w2_{ij} = \begin{cases} \sum\limits_{k=1}^{m} wa_{ik} & i = j \\ 0 & otherwise \end{cases}$$

$$d1_{ij} = \begin{cases} \sum\limits_{j=1}^{n} ws_{ij} \cdot \dfrac{ds_{ij}}{\overline{ds}_{ij}^{\,old}} & i = j,\ \overline{ds}_{ij}^{\,old} \neq 0 \\ -ws_{ij} \cdot \dfrac{ds_{ij}}{\overline{ds}_{ij}^{\,old}} & i,\ \overline{ds}_{ij}^{\,old} \neq 0 \\ 0 & otherwise \end{cases} \tag{10}$$

$$d2_{ij} = \begin{cases} \sum\limits_{k=1}^{m} wa_{ik} \cdot \dfrac{da_{ik}}{\overline{da}_{ik}^{\,old}} & i = j,\ \overline{da}_{ik}^{\,old} \neq 0 \\ 0 & otherwise \end{cases}$$

$$d3_{ik} = \begin{cases} wa_{ik} \cdot \dfrac{da_{ik}}{\overline{da}_{ik}^{\,old}} & \overline{da}_{ik}^{\,old} \neq 0 \\ 0 & otherwise \end{cases}$$

From (9), we can get:

$$S^{new} = inv(W1 + W2) \cdot \left[(D1 + D2) \cdot S^{old} + (WA - D3) \cdot A\right] \tag{11}$$

Equation (11) is the neighborhood function which only use the distances between neighbor nodes to generate a new solution from an old solution.

3.2 Greedy Optimization Localization Algorithm

To obtain an accurate localization result, GOLA includes two correction operations to alleviate the flip ambiguity.

The GOLA pseudo code is shown in Algorithm 1.

Algorithm 1
1. Start($maxNum, p$)
2.   Load the known data like A, R, WA, WS, DA, DS;
3. $finalSolution$ = null;
4. $minCV$ = inf;
5.   for $i = 1{:}p$
6. S^{old} = randomly generate an initial solution;
7. $CF_{old} = comCF(S^{old}, \cdots)$;
8. $CF_{new} = CF_{old}$; $k = 0$; $S^{new} = S^{old}$;
9.   while $k == 0$ ($CF_{old} - CF_{new} > 0 \&\& k \le maxNum$)
10. $k = k+1$; $CF_{old} = CF_{new}$; $S^{old} = S^{new}$;
11. $S^{new} = comNewSolution(S^{old}, \cdots)$;
12. $CF_{new} = comCF(S^{new}, \cdots)$;
13.   end
14. $S_{old} = S_{new}$;
15. $[S_{new}, leavingNode] = correctionOne(S^{old}, \cdots)$;
16.   if $leavingNode \ne 0$
17. $S_{old} = S_{new}$;
18. $S_{new} = correctionTwo(S^{old}, \cdots)$;
19.   end
20. $CV_{new} = comCV(S^{new}, \cdots)$;
21.   if $CV_{new} < minCV$
22. $finalSolution = S^{new}$;
23. $minCV = CV_{new}$;
24.   end
25.   end

4   Performance Evaluation

In this section, simulations are conducted using MATLAB to evaluate the performance of GOLA and compare GOLA with Multilateration [19], MDS-MAP [20] and PAES [24]. To investigate the impact of a concave area on the performance of Multilateration, MDS-MAP, PAES and GOLA, we use two scenes shown in Fig. 1.

Circles represent anchors and asterisks represent non-anchors. In the first scene, 200 non-anchors are randomly deployed in a 100×100 m^2 square area (i.e., a convex area) as shown in Fig. 1(a). In the second scene, 200 non-anchors are randomly deployed in a 100×100 m^2 area with a coverage hole (i.e., a concave area) as shown in Fig. 1(b). The number of anchors m and R will be given in later tests.

The distances between neighbor nodes can be measured by hardware or calculated by distance estimation algorithms. In this paper, distances are generated according to

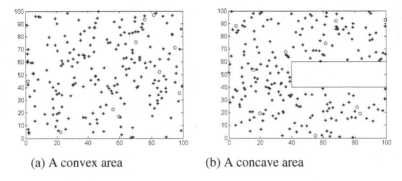

(a) A convex area   (b) A concave area

Fig. 1. Two network environments

Eq. (1). The distance error is determined by α. To evaluate the performance of algorithms, we use the mean error between the estimated and real locations of non-anchors, defined as follows:

$$LE = \frac{1}{nR} \cdot \sum_{i=1}^{n} \sqrt{(x_i - \bar{x}_i)^2 + (y_i - \bar{y}_i)^2} \times 100\,\% \qquad (12)$$

where LE denotes the localization error; n is the number of the non-anchors (n is 200 in this paper). R is the communication radius. (x_i, y_i) and $(\bar{x}_i, \bar{y}_i)$ respectively denote the true and estimated locations of a non-anchor i. In this paper, *maxNum* of GOLA is 2000 in Algorithm 1.

4.1   Impact of Different Initial Solution on LE

As we mentioned before, GOLA is a local optimization algorithm. The localization result completely depends on the initial solution when the neighborhood function is fixed. We design two ways of generating the initial solution. One way, denoted by different-location, is that initial locations of all non-anchors are in different random locations. The other, denoted by same-location, is that initial locations of all non-anchors are in the same random location. To investigate the impact of different initial solutions on LE of GOLA, we test 10 different initial solutions generated by each way. We set $R = 20$ m, 10 anchors and $\alpha = 0.1$ in Eq. (1). The comparison results are shown in Fig. 2. Figure 2(a) shows that the simulation results in a convex area, and the average LE of 10 different initial solutions generated by same-location is 4.02 % and the average LE of different-location is 7.91 %. Figure 2(b) shows the simulation results in a concave area, and the average LE of same-location is 5.05 % and the average LE of same-location is 9.12 %. It is clear that the LE of same-location is smaller than the LE of different-location in both a convex area and a concave area. Hence, we use the same-location way to generate the initial solution in later tests. We note that different initial solutions obtained by the same-location way generate different LEs. The reason is that GOLA is a local search algorithm.

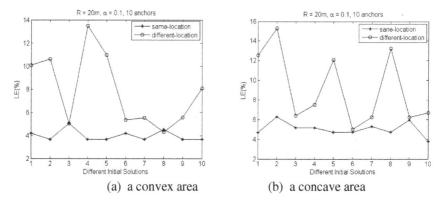

(a) a convex area   (b) a concave area

Fig. 2. Impact of different initial solutions on LE of GOLA

In order to get accurate estimated locations, GOLA is performed p times with different initial solutions to generate p different local optimal solutions. Then we choose the final solution by the lowest value of CV in Eq. (12). Table 1 shows the values of CV corresponding to LEs represented as the asterisks in Fig. 2.

Table 1. LEs and the values of CV

Simulation round	Convex area		Concave area	
	LE	CV	LE	CV
1	4.18	186	4.67	258
2	3.66	178	6.27	368
3	5.34	262	5.18	300
4	3.52	168	5.05	292
5	3.80	182	4.7	262
6	4.18	186	4.73	264
7	3.66	178	5.30	308
8	4.52	214	4.74	270
9	3.69	180	5.94	344
10	3.62	174	3.79	212

In Table 1, we can see that the LE is direct ratio to the value of CV. This demonstrates it is effective to choose the final solution by the lowest value of CV.

To obtain more accurate estimated locations, we design a method of generating initial solutions: we divide the deployed area into k small sub-regions with the equal area (e.g., 16, 25, 50, etc.). We generate a random location in each small sub-region as an initial solution (note that an initial solution is generated by same-location way). Then we can obtain p initial solutions. We use the p initial solutions to generate p different local optimal solutions and choose the final solution by the lowest value of CV. The more sub-regions we divide the area into, the more initial solutions we

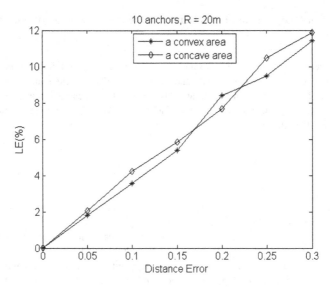

Fig. 3. Impact of distance error on LEs of GOLA

will get. Meanwhile, the more initial solutions we get, the more accurate estimated locations we will obtain.

4.1.1 Impact of Distance Error on LE of GOLA

As mentioned in Eq. (1), distances between neighbor nodes have distance error no matter how to get distances between neighbor nodes. In this simulation, we set 10 anchors and communication range $R = 20$ m. The parameter of distance error α in Eq. (1) is changed from 0 to 0.3. Figure 3 shows the simulation results. It is clear that the LE of GOLA increases as the distance error increases. When $\alpha = 0$ (i.e., the distance error is 0), the LE of GOLA in a convex is 0.01 % and the LE of GOLA in a concave is 0.02 %.

We can see the LE of GOLA is very small when the distance is accurate in both scenes. Furthermore, the LE of GOLA in a concave area is a little higher than the LE of GOLA in a convex area in most case.

5 Conclusion

In this paper, we analyze existing localization algorithms for WSNs in a concave area and find that the shortest path may deviate far away from straight lines and lead to inaccurate localization results. To solve the problem, a novel localization algorithm is proposed. First, we make a deep analysis on the distance relation between two successive estimated locations of non-anchors on the assumption that the new estimated locations are correct. Then we design a novel neighborhood function, which only uses the distances between neighbor nodes to generate a new set of estimated locations from an old set of estimated locations. Finally, we test performance of GOLA; simulation results show that GOLA is an efficient and reliable localization algorithm for wireless sensor network.

Acknowledgements. This work was supported by National Natural Science Foundation of China (60903159, 61173153), the Science and Technology Plan of Shenyang (1091176-1-00), the Special Fund from the Central Collegiate Basic Scientific Research Bursary (N110818001, N100218001) and a new technology of broadband wireless mobile communication network projects (2013ZX03002006).

References

1. Cheng, L., Wu, C.D., Zhang, Y.Z.: A survey of localization in wireless sensor network. Int. J. Distrib. Sens. Netw. **2012**(962523), 13 (2012)
2. Han, G.J., Jiang, J.F., Shu, L., Xu, Y.J., Wang, F.: Localization algorithms of underwater wireless sensor networks: a survey. Sensors **12**(2), 2026–2061 (2012)
3. Redondi, A., Chirico, M., Borsani, L.: An integrated system based on wireless sensor networks for patient monitoring, localization and tracking. AD Hoc Netw. **11**(1), 39–53 (2013)
4. Chen, X., Zhang, B.L.: Improved DV-Hop node localization algorithm in wireless sensor networks. Int. J. Distrib. Sens. Netw. **2012**(213980), 8 (2012)
5. Xie, P., Cui, J.H., Lao, L.: VBF: vector-based forwarding protocol for underwater sensor networks. In: Proceedings of the IFIP Networking, pp. 1216–1221. Lisbon, Portugal (2006)
6. Chen, C.C., Chang, C.Y., Li, Y.N.: Range-free localization scheme in wireless sensor networks based on bilateration. Int. J. Distrib. Sens. Netw. **2013**(620248), 10 (2013)
7. Bulusu, N., Heidemann, J., Estrin, D.: GPS-less low-cost outdoor localization for very small devices. IEEE Pers. Commun. **7**(5), 28–34 (2000)
8. Bulusu, N., Heidemann, J.: Adaptive beacon placement. In: Proceedings of the 21st IEEE International Conference on Distributed Computing Systems, Mesa (AZ), pp. 489–498 (2001)
9. He, T., Huang, C.D, Blum, B.M., Stankovic, J.A., Abdelzaher, T.: Range-free localization schemes for large scale sensor networks. In: Proceedings of the 9th ACM on Mobile Computing and Networking, California (UAS), pp. 81–95 (2003)
10. Sun, S.Y., Zhu, S.H., Ding, Z.G.: TOA-based source localization: a linearization approach adopting coordinate system translation. Int. J. Distrib. Sens. Netw. **2013**(379369), 7 (2013)
11. Weng, Y., Xiao, W., Xie, L.: Total least squares method for robust source localization in sensor networks using TDOA measurements. Int. J. Distrib. Sens. Netw. **2011**(172902), 8 (2011)
12. Ho, K.C.: Bias reduction for an explicit solution of source localization using TDOA. IEEE Trans. Signal Process. **60**(5), 2101–2114 (2012)
13. Lee, Y.S., Park, J.W., Barolli, L.: A localization algorithm based on AOA for ad-hoc sensor networks. Mob. Inf. Syst. **8**(1), 61–72 (2012)
14. Moravek, P., Komosny, D., Simek, M., Gribau, D.: Energy analysis of received signal strength localization in wireless sensor networks. Radioengineering **20**(4), 937–945 (2011)
15. Niculescu, D., Nath, B.: Ad hoc positioning system (APS). In: Proceedings of IEEE Global Telecommunications Conference (GLOBECOM 2001), vol. 5, San Antonio, TX, USA, pp. 2926–2931 (2001)

16. Wu, G., Wang, S., Wang, B., Dong, Y., Yan, S.: A novel range-free localization based on regulated neighborhood distance for wireless ad hoc and sensor networks. Comput. Netw. **56** (16), 3581–3593 (2012)

17. Zhong, Z.G., He, T.: RSD: A metric for achieving range-free localization beyond connectivity. IEEE Trans. Parallel Distrib. Syst. **22**(11), 1943–1951 (2011)

18. Wang, Y., Wang, X.D., Wang, D.M., Dharma, P.: Range-free localization using expected hop progress in wireless sensor networks. IEEE Trans. Parallel Distrib. Syst. **20**(10), 1540–1552 (2009)

19. Savvides, A., Park, H., Srivastava, M.B.: The bits and flops of the n-hop multilateration primitive for node localization problems. In: Proceedings of the ACM International Workshop on Wireless Sensor Networks and Applications, New York, USA, pp. 112–121 (2002)

20. Shang, Y., Wheeler, R., Zhang, Y.: Localization from mere connectivity. In: Proceedings of the 4th ACM International Symposium on Mobile ad Hoc Networking & Computing, Annapolis, Maryland, USA, pp. 201–212 (2003)

21. Shang, Y., Shi, H., Ahmed, A.: Performance study of localization algorithms in ad-hoc sensor networks. In: Proceedings of the IEEE International Conference on Mobile Ad Hoc and Sensor System, pp. 184–193 (2004)

22. Lim, H., Hou, J.C.: Localization for anisotropic sensor networks. In: Proceedings of the Annual Joint Conference of the IEEE Computer and Communications Societies, vol. 1, pp. 138–149 (2005)

23. Shon, M., Jo, M., Choo, H.: An interactive cluser-based MDS localization scheme for multimedia information in wireless sensor networks. Comput. Commun. **35**(15), 1921–1929 (2012)

24. Kannan, A.A., Mao, G.Q., Vucetic, B.: Simulated annealing based wireless sensor network localization with flip ambiguity mitigation. In: Proceedings of the IEEE 63rd Vehicular Technology Conference, 2006, VTC 2006-Spring, Melbourne, vol. 2, pp. 1022–1026 (2006)

25. Massimo, V., Roberto, L.V., Francesco, M.: A two-objective evolutionary approach based on topological constraints for node localization in wireless sensor networks. Appl. Soft Comput. **12**(7), 1891–1901 (2012)

Multi-dimensional Forwarding Tables

Gautier Bayzelon[1], Shu Yang[2]($\boxtimes$), Mingwei Xu[1], and Qi Li[2]

[1] Tsinghua University, Beijing, China
[2] Graduate School at Shenzhen, Tsinghua University,
Room 205, Building H, Beijing 518055, China
yang.shu@sz.tsinghua.edu.cn

Abstract. Traditional networks make routing decisions based only on the destination address. This dramatically limits the number of ser-vices that a network can provide. However, in some of them, the demand for more flexible routing protocols has increased. For example, home and enterprise networks, as well as datacenters, need to support multi-homing and/or role-based access control. This is where two-dimensional forwarding tables step in. In this approach, routing decisions are based on the destination and the source addresses. However, this will increase the lookup time and make the memory use skyrocket if implemented carelessly. In this paper, we evaluate and compare different designs to find the best way to tackle this problem.

1 Introduction

The single destination address information is no longer sufficient to manage networks and data centres [1], set access control lists, firewalls [2] etc. The introduction of the source address (and even maybe the flow label) would considerably broaden the range of possibilities and give operators more freedom in implementing policies. There are many solutions to support these policies. For example, policy-based routing (PBR) [3] installs policies into access control list (ACL), and multi-topology routing (MTR) [4] supports multiple independent control and forwarding planes. Currently, engineers in IETF are proposing traffic-class routing (TCR) [5,6] that adds more information, e.g., source address, into routing, such that routing decisions can be made based on both destination and source addresses.

Although these solutions differ greatly in control plane; they all need an enhanced forwarding plane to support large number of forwarding rules based on an increasing number of routing policies. Nevertheless, current solutions are not scalable. For example, MTR uses a separate forwarding table for each topology, but it can only support a limited number (32 in most cases [4]) of topologies while current enterprise networks require more [7]; TCR recommends using one forwarding table per source prefix. This scales even worse than MTR and is only suitable for small networks.

However, the addition of this new piece of information will also increase the size of the tables/lists and increase lookup times. Therefore we have to think

© Springer-Verlag Berlin Heidelberg 2015
S. Zhang et al. (Eds.): ICoC 2014, CCIS 502, pp. 68–79, 2015.
DOI: 10.1007/978-3-662-46826-5_6

about new designs to include this new data while keeping the lookup time as short as possible and the memory use to a reasonable extent.

In this paper, we propose and compare different designs to tackle this problem. We will detail and examine several trie-based designs. Then we will test the performances of each design by measuring the time required to build a table from an input text file. We will also measure the size of the table, as well as the lookup and updating time.

2 Background

We first present some background on hardware packet processing in a router. We show a common implementation in Fig. 1. After a packet arrives on a router, it will traverse the datapath on a linecard, which include ACL (Access Control List), PBR (Policy Based Routing) and finally FIB. ACL and PBR are used for different levels of packet classification, and mostly implemented at powerful edge routers. In some implementations, ACL and PBR are merged into one module [8] and some simple routers only have FIB. The key that there are so many separated modules instead of one FIB is that we do need packet classification, yet the complexity of packet classification makes it difficult for FIB to support them directly. Therefore, the FIB is made up with only destination-based prefixes, and ACL and PBR contains necessary classification rules. If a packet matches the rules in ACL or PBR, they will be filtered (or handed in to control plane for further processing) and forwarded. Otherwise, it goes to the FIB for destination-based forwarding. The conventional FIB structure is shown in Fig. 2(a). The prefixes are stored in TCAM and the nexthop actions are stored in SRAM.

Clearly, if we may build more routing semantics into FIB itself, it makes the router logically more sound, and possibly less messier of the rules in the ACL/PBR modules. In this paper, we study multi-dimensional forwarding table by including source address and other fields into the FIB.

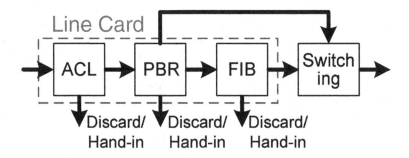

Fig. 1. The datapath that packets traverse

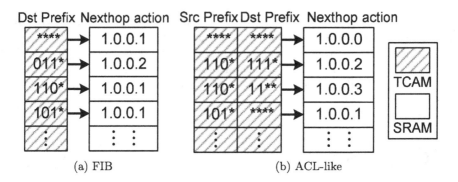

(a) FIB   (b) ACL-like

Fig. 2. Conventional FIB and ACL-like structures

3 Related Work

Several solutions have already been suggested to answer the increasing demand of users and applications for better services. Many research works focus on new routing solutions, e.g., PBR [3], MTR [4], TCR [5,9] and recent software-defined network (SDN). In layer-3, more and more routing schemes make routing decisions based on both source and destination addresses, such as policy routing [10], NIRA [11], customer-specific routing [12], Destination/Source routing [13].

The simplest extension to support rich policies is using multiple one dimensional forwarding tables [4,5], However, this solution does not scale. Improved solutions can be divided into two broad categories: CAM-based and algorithmic solutions [14]. Here, we focus on CAM-based solutions.

CAM-based, especially TCAM-based solutions are the de facto standard in industry. However, TCAM-based solutions are limited by its capacity [15]. What is worse, TCAM is highly customized, there are limited techniques we can use to compress it. The most popular technique is aggregation [16,17]. The largest TCAM chips available currently are still rather limited in memory storage. In 2011, it could only accommodate 1 million IPv4 prefixes [15] and therefore is not enough to store the entire two-dimensional table in IPv6 [18].

More works are proposed for algorithmic solutions, such as trie-based, decision-tree, and bitmap-based approaches [14]. However, they suffer from non-deterministic performance and do not scale well [19]. Bit-vector linear search [20] performs individual lookups in each dimension, each dimension will output a $O(n)$ length vector representing matched rules. By interseting bit-vectors, the algorithm computes the final result. Cross-producting [21] extracts the elements in each dimension, and stores all combinations in a database.

Some researches have also already been done on multi-dimensional routing [14,22,23] and ACL compression [17,24]. Most of them use set-pruning tries and grid of tries. The last architecture is actually a trie that uses switch pointers between sub-tries. It is the one that gives the best performances so far but the only drawback is that the update algorithm is quite heavy. More details can be found in [14].

4   The Designs

4.1   One FIB per Source Prefix Plus a General One

This first implementation is a slightly modified version of the one introduced in
F.J. Baker's draft [9]. As it is said in the title, we will have one forwarding table
for each source prefix and a general table for rules that do not specify any source
(i.e. the traditional rules). When adding a new route to this architecture, there
are two pos-sibilities. First case: the source prefix of the new route is specified.
Then we obviously add the route to the associated FIB. If there is no such FIB,
we create one. Second case: if the source prefix of the new route is unspecified,
we store it in the general FIB.

When forwarding a packet, we look at its source address to determine which
FIB we should use. If it is from one of the configured prefixes, we look the destination up in the indicated FIB. In any event, we also look in the "unspecified
source address" FIB. If the destination is found in only one of the two, the indicated route is followed. If the destination is found in both, the more specific route
is followed. The most specific route is the one with the most specific destination
prefix.

Then comes the question of how to deal with ambiguities, which was not considered in the draft. An ambiguity occurs when there are two routes $< dp, sp, A >$
and $< dp', sp', B >$ such as dp (the destination prefix) is more specific than dp'
but sp (the source prefix) is less specific than sp'. A and B or the decisions associated. The traffic class $< dp, sp' >$ matches both rules so in theory, we could
either chose A or B. This is why there is an ambiguity. If we want to give the
priority to the destination [5] upon the source, there are two possibilities. The
first one is to modify the "add" algorithm. Instead of adding a route only to
the FIB that has the same source prefix, we also add it to every FIB for which
the source prefix is more specific. Note that we also have to keep trace of these
added routes in case at some point, the original one is deleted. Of course we have
to delete these added route as well but we need a way to distinguish them from
the ones that purely belong to the specific table. The obvious problem of this
solution is that if we have two FIB, X and Y, such as the source prefix associated
to Y is more specific than the one associated to X, all the rules in X will have to
be added to Y. We will therefore waste memory. This scenario may be neglected
in small networks because ambiguities are unlikely to happen there. However, it
makes this design not very suitable to wider networks. This is the solution that
we implemented. Another way to deal with ambiguities is to modify the lookup
algorithm. Instead of only looking for the route up in the FIB with the most
specific source prefix, we look in every FIB for which the source address of the
datagram matches the associated source prefix. This way, we save memory space
but we slow down the lookup time.

In conclusion, the great advantage of this approach is its simplicity. The
argument against it is that it is memory-hungry and the lookups may not be very
fast as the rules are stored using vectors.

4.2   The Slicing Design

This design is inspired from F.J. Baker's draft and has been improved. We consider the destination and the source prefixes as bit strings. If we compare all the destination strings (respectively the source strings) with one another, we can differentiate three regions: common, varying and ignored region. For example, if we have two prefixes 00* and 01*, the first bit is common, the second one is varying and everything from the third bit is ignored. This approach makes sense because all global IPv6 addresses at this writing are within 2000::/3, so while these three bits must be tested to assure a match, doing a classification on them is useless as they are the same for all the prefixes. The varying part is where there are some differences between the strings and the ignored parts are the ones that are not covered by the mask. This is the basic idea. We then modified the node structure, the trie construction algorithm and created our own update algorithm to improve the perfor-mances of the design.

The trie is constructed by recursive slice-wise decomposition. At each stage, the input is a set of traffic classes to be classified. The output is a node identifying the type of its slices (destination or source), its constant slice (starting bit, length and value), its varying slice (starting bit and length) and a set of classes to be classified. If this previous set is empty, it means we have reached a leaf of the trie. If not, we analyse the set in a similar manner. If one or more bits in the slice is/are ignored in some classes, those classes must be included in every subset. If all the input classes have only common and ignored parts, we stop and keep only the most specific one. Last but not least, as we want to give the priority to the destination, we start from there.

Figure 1 is an example of how the trie would be built if the input traffic classes were:

A = dst=2001:db8::/32, src=2001:db8:3::/48
B = dst=2001:db8:0::/48, src=2001:db8:2::/48
C = dst=2001:db8:1::/48, src=::/0

Of course, the varying slice does not have to be only one bit. We did so in order to keep things "readable".

To lookup something up in the trie, we start at the root and compare the constant part. If it does not match, we discard the datagram, as there is no matching rule for its address. Otherwise we go to the appropriate child considering the varying part and start the process again until we reach a leaf.

Updating the trie is, however, a little complex. When adding a new rule, we start from the root of the trie and compare the common part. If it is the same, we go to the appropriate child or children and start the process again. Indeed, we have to add the rule to several children if the varying part identified by the node is not entirely covered by the rule, exactly the same way as it is done during the construction algorithm. If the common part is different or ignored by the new rule, we have to consider all the rules that were used as an input to build the actual node, add the new rule to this set and start the classification again from there.

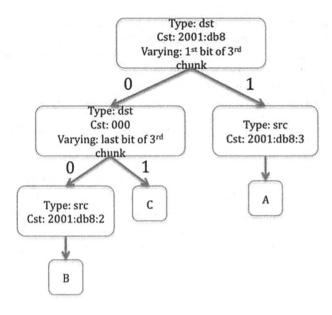

Fig. 3. Discontinuous trie construction

The advantage of this method is that it avoids "useless" classification (cf example with the prefixes starting with 2000::/3). We can also compare groups of bits instead of just doing bit-to-bit comparison, which allow us to save some time during a lookup. Indeed, the smallest data unit manageable is a byte so comparing 8 bits or only one, takes the same amount of time. The default is probably that it is a little complex to build if we want the size of the varying slice to change. Adding rules is also pretty heavy as there are a lot of particular cases. Most of the time, it is enough to just introduce an intermediate node in the trie but in some cases, it is much more complex. Another default may be that, when applied to a larger network with a lot of rules, a lot of nodes may have no common parts. Therefore, we would be wasting space by storing the null common part attributes.

For the simulation, we first used varying slices of one bit and then one byte. Note that the common part length, in both cases, can vary from zero to several bytes.

5   Evaluation Metrics and Environment

It is quite difficult to express the memory and time complexity of the different designs with literal expressions as both of them depend on the "similarity" between the rules. For example, are there rules more specific than others or are they all different? Does the first chunk of IP address contain most of the differences? Therefore we run these algorithms in practice and compare the results.

The simulation was done on a laptop with a 2.4 GHz processor. The objective of the experiment was to simulate the Chinese network and divert the traffic that was going from Tsinghua University (Beijing) and toward the outside world, to Shanghai. Therefore, we extracted a set of rules from the CERNET2 network. There were 6936 rules in total, all destination based. Then to divert the traffic from Tsinghua University, we created another set of rules by combining all the prefixes associated to the University (38 in total) to all the prefixes for the foreign networks (6355). Therefore, the second set was composed of 38 * 6355 = 241 490 multi-dimensional rules in total. Adding the two sets of rules, we have 248 426 rules as an input in a text file.

We then measured the time the algorithm took to build the entire two-dimensional table and sized the memory space used. Once the table was built, we also measured the lookup speed for different values of the destination and source addresses. Finally, we determined the update time when adding or deleting a rule, which is a critical point as the update frequency on connec-tivity information can reach tens of thou-sands per second in actual networks [25].

6   Simulation

We ran the tests several times and computed the average for each metrics. For the sake of clarity, we will refer to the "one FIB per source prefix plus a general one" design as algorithm 1 and to the slicing algorithms explained in part 3.2 as 2 and 3 (one-bit varying slice and one byte-varying slice respectively). Table 1 gathers the results for the three designs and for all the metrics. Figure 2 also brings a more visual representation of the results.

6.1   Building Time

We build the forwarding table from scratch several time and measure how long it takes. On average, it is slightly faster to build it with the "one-FIB-per-source-prefix-plus-a-general-one" (referred to as algorithm 1) as it takes around 60 seconds. The "varying-size key lookup tries" (afterwards, referred to as algorithm 2 for the one-bit varying slice and 3 for the one-byte varying slice) take approximately 65 seconds.

The first algorithm is faster than the two others because it requires less comparison to build the table(s).

6.2   Memory Complexity

Once the table is built, we count the number of necessary bytes to store it. Once again, the first design is the best. We found that, without any level-compression algorithm, the table produced by algorithm 2 is 4.2 times bigger. This is explained by the fact that the size of every varying slice is one bit. However, the smallest data unit that we can store is one byte, therefore,

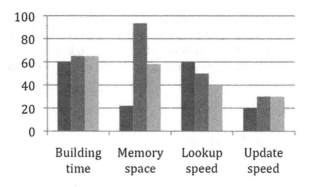

Fig. 4. Evaluation results

Table 1. Evaluation results

	Building Time	Memory Space	Lookup Speed	Update Speed
1	60	21.9	60	20
2	65	93.5	50	30
3	65	58.2	40	30

we are wasting seven bits every time we make a classification. This can be greatly improved even by using a very simple compression algorithm. For example, we could detect all the nodes for which the varying slices are consecutive and merge them into a single node with a wider varying slice. Smarter algorithms may be designed in the future to compress the table with a greater efficiency [26]. The third algorithm produces a table 2.6 times bigger than the first one. The difference in sizes also comes from the fact that the tries use a lot of pointers, which are not so light compared to the size of the data that a node has to store (Fig. 4).

6.3   Lookup Speed

To compare the designs, we made 500 000 lookups and study the average time. The lookups were made using the rules used to build the different FIBs. As the first design uses vector to store the rules, we also made sure that the rules we were looking up, were equally spread in the vectors. This time we see that the ranking changed. The third algorithm becomes the best thanks to its classification, followed by the second algorithm, which makes the first design the slowest.

6.4   Add/Delete/Update Route Speed

Once the table is built, we added and deleted 20,000 routes and measure the time it took to update the tables. First we added ten thousand "destination only" routes. That is, the source prefix is unspecified. This was done almost instantly in all cases. Then we added two-dimensional rules. This time however, the performances of the first algorithm did not change, but the second and third algorithms took a little longer because again, more comparisons were involved.

7   Case Study

To test the load that multi-dimensional forwarding table brings to the network. We test the forwarding table in a testbed as shown in Fig. 3. The testbed is composed of 5 PCs (with Intel Xeon E5504). Among them, 4 PCs acts as routers, and run Quagga as control plane, and Click as forwarding plane. The other PC acts as the source host, which sends packets to the network, through packet-capture function on each PC, we can obtain the traveling path of each packet.

In this case, we want to simulate the scenario in CERNET2, where R_2 and R_3 represents the out-going routers in CERNET2, e.g., R_2 corresponds to the router in Beijing, R_3 corresponds to the router in Shanghai. Thus, we divert the designated traffic from three universities from Beijing to Shanghai. Thus, with traditional routing protocol and forwarding table, the traffic will flow from R_1 to R_2. With a new two dimensional routing protocol and a new two dimensional forwarding table follow the structure of one FIB per source prefix plus a general one, the traffic will flow from R_1 to either R_2 or R_3, depends on the source address.

In Fig. 6, we can see that the CPU utilization of traditional destination-based routing and two dimensional routing. We can see that in most time, the CPU utilization for two dimensional routing/forwarding is roughly the same with destination-based routing/forwarding. The CPU utilization will reach a peak periodically, because of running routing algorithms. Thus, we can conclude that the two dimensional routing/forwarding in this case does not bring much CPU loads, current routers has enough capacity to process the additional loads.

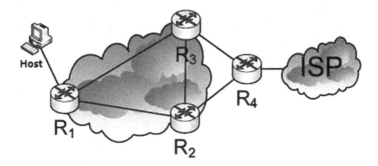

Fig. 5. Testbed environment

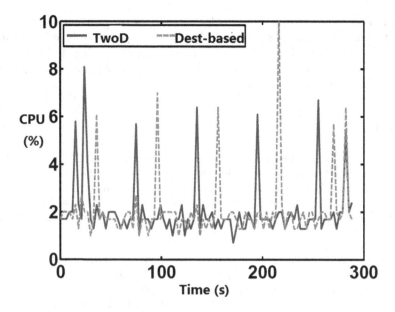

Fig. 6. CPU utilization of router R_1 in Fig. 5

8   Discussion

We see that there is necessarily a trade-off between memory use and speed. We can make the following improvements in the future.

- We could reduce the memory needed by algorithm 2 and 3 by using level-compression and trie-folding algorithms. There are also some identical subtries especially for the first design (all the tables attached to a source prefix are the same). Instead of having several copies of them, we could just have several pointers pointing to the same one. However, this may add another difficulty to the update algorithm.
- We could combine the algorithmic solutions with CAM-based solutions, such that the hardware can provide fast linecard lookup speed, and the algorithm can improve the storage space.

9   Conclusion

We have see and compared different possible designs to store two-dimensional forwarding tables. These designs could relatively easily be extended to more dimensions if needed. Moreover, although each one of these architectures can be improved, there is probably not an absolute best design, as we always have to juggle between memory space and lookup or update speed. However, we can reasonably assume that the number of source prefixes will be a lot smaller than the number of destination prefixes. Therefore, we could imagine a design where we would first have a size-varying key lookup trie for the destination. The leaves of this trie would then point to arrays that would store the source information. Or we could even use the slicing design to only store the first 4 chunks of the destination prefixes and then vectors for the rest. These kind of architectures should be studied in future works.

References

1. Kim, H., Claffy, K., Fomenkov, M., Barman, D., Faloutsos, M., Lee, K.: Internet traffic classification demystified: myths, caveats, and the best practices. In: Porceedings of ACM CoNEXT'08, Madrid, Spain, December 2008
2. Acharya, S., Wang, J., Ge, Z., Znati, T., Greenberg, A.: Simulation study of firewalls to aid improved performance. In: 39th Annual Simulation Symposium, April 2006
3. Cisco: Policy-Based Routing (white paper) (1996)
4. Juniper: Multi-topology Routing (white paper), August 2010
5. Baker, F.: IPv6 Source/Destination Routing using OSPFv3 Feb 2013. Internet Draft. www.draft-baker-ipv6-ospf-dst-src-routing-00
6. Lindem, A., Mirtorabi, S., Roy, A., Baker, F.: Ospfv3 LSA Extendibility May 2013. Internet Draft. www.draft-acee-ospfv3-lsa-extend-01
7. Benson, T., Akella, A., Maltz, D.A.: Mining policies from enterprise network configuration. In: Proceedings of ACM IMC'09, Chicago, IL, November 2009
8. Gupta, P.: Algorithms for routing lookups and packet classification. Ph.D. thesis, Stanford University (2000)
9. Baker, F.: Routing a Traffic Class January 2012. Internet Draft. www.draft-baker-fun-routing-class-00
10. Seehra, A., Naous, J., Walfish, M., Mazires, D., Nicolosi, A., Shenker, S.: A policy framework for the future internet. In: Proceedings of ACM HotNets'09, New York, October 2009
11. Yang, X., Clark, D., Berger, A.W.: Nira: a new inter-domain routing architecture. IEEE/ACM Trans. Netw. 15(4), 775–788 (2007)
12. Fu J., Rexford, J.: Efficient ip-address lookup with a shared forwarding table for multiple virtual routers. In: Proceedings of ACM CoNEXT 2008, Madrid, Spain, December 2008
13. Lamparter, D.: Destination/source Routing Oct 2014. Internet Draft. www.draft-lamparter-rtgwg-dst-src-routing-00.txt
14. Varghese, G.: Network Algorithmics: An Interdisciplinary Approach to Designing Fast Networked Devices. Morgan Kaufmann, Waltham (2005)
15. Meiners, C.R., Liu, A.X., Torng, E., Patel, J.: Split: optimizing space, power, and throughput for tcam-based classification. In: Proceedings of ACM/IEEE ANCS 2011, Brooklyn, NY, October 2011
16. Liu, A., Meiners, C., Torng, E.: Tcam razor: A systematic approach towards minimizing packet classifiers in tcams. Netw., IEEE/ACM Trans. 18(2), 490–500 (2010)
17. Meiners, C., Liu, A., Torng, E.: Bit weaving: a non-prefix approach to compressing packet classifiers in tcams. In: Proceedings of IEEE ICNP 2009, Orlando, Florida, October 2009
18. Meiners, C., Liu, A., Torng, E.: Hardware Based Packet Classification for High Speed Internet Routers. Springer, New York (2010)

19. Ma, Y., Banerjee, S.: A smart pre-classifier to reduce power consumption of tcams for multi-dimensional packet classification. In: Proceedings of ACM SIGCOMM 2012, Helsinki, Finland, August 2012
20. Lakshman, T.V., Stiliadis, D.: High-speed policy-based packet forwarding using efficient multi-dimensional range matching. SIGCOMM Comput. Commun. Rev. **28**(4), 203–214 (1998)
21. Srinivasan, V., Varghese, G., Suri, S., Waldvogel, M.: Fast and scalable layer four switching. In: Proceeding of ACM SIGCOMM 1998, Vancouver, British Columbia, Canada, August 1998
22. Chang, Y.-K.: Efficient multidimensional packet classification with fast updates. IEEE Trans. Comput. **58**(4), 463–479 (2009)
23. Qi, Y., Xu, L., Yang, B., Xue, Y., Li, J.: Packet classification algorithms: from theory to practice. In: Proceedings of IEEE Infocom 2009, Rio de Janeiro, Brazil, April 2009
24. Suri, S., Sandholm, T., Warkhede, P.: Compressing two-dimensional routing tables. Algorithmica **35**, 287–300 (2003)
25. Mishra, T., Sahni, S.: Duos - simple dual tcam architecture for routing tables with incremental update. In: Proceedings of IEEE ISCC 2010, Riccione, Italy, June 2010
26. Rétvári, G., Tapolcai, J., Kőrösi, A., Majdán, A., Heszberger, Z.: Compressing ip forwarding tables: towards entropy bounds and beyond. In: Proceedings of the ACM SIGCOMM 2013 Conference on SIGCOMM, SIGCOMM 2013 (2013)

Performance Evaluation of Routing Schemes in Data Center Clos Networks

Yi Wang, Chen Tian$^{(\boxtimes)}$, Shengjun Wang, and Wenyu Liu

School of Electronic Information and Communications,
Huazhong University of Science and Technology,
Wuhan, Hubei, People's Republic of China
{ywang,tianchen,sjwang,liuwy}@hust.edu.cn
http://ei.hust.edu.cn

Abstract. A number of new Clos data center networking fabrics have been proposed recently by using commodity off-the-shelf hardware. In Clos networks, randomized routing is typically used to achieve load balance. However, with typical communication patterns, pure randomized routing design cannot fully exploit bandwidth provided by Clos topologies. This paper strives to evaluate the performance of both randomized routing and its alternatives. As an incremental improvement, periodic path renewal is discussed first. We then discuss adaptive routing, together with its implementation consideration and costs. To reduce overhead of pure adaptive routing, a mixed routing scheme is also discussed. Through detailed discussions and comprehensive evaluations, we provide designers with useful insight and a range of options for configuring the routing scheme.

Keywords: Clos network · Routing · Data center networks

1 Introduction

Cloud services are driving the creation of gigantic data centers which can concurrently satisfy computing and storage needs for many global businesses. Running distributed file systems (e.g. GFS) and distributed programming models (e.g. MapReduce and Dryad), these gigantic data centers may hold millions of servers in the near future. Unfortunately, existing multi-rooted-tree-like network fabrics cannot economically provide enough bisectional throughput among the servers of large data centers. The nearer to the root of a tree topology, the higher the cost of the switches/routers hardware. As a consequence, the capacity between

Yi Wang—This work is partially supported by "National Natural Science Foundation of China (No. 61202107, No. 61100220, No. 61202303)", by "National High Technology Research and Development Program of China (863 Program No. 2014AA01A702)", by "Natural Science Foundation of Hubei Province (No. 2014CFB1007), and by "National Key Technology Research and Development Program of China (No. 2012BAH46F03)".

© Springer-Verlag Berlin Heidelberg 2015
S. Zhang et al. (Eds.): ICoC 2014, CCIS 502, pp. 80–94, 2015.
DOI: 10.1007/978-3-662-46826-5_7

different branches of the tree topology is typically oversubscribed by factors from 1:5 to 1:240 [8].

To solve this problem, a number of new data center networking fabrics have been proposed recently by using commodity off-the-shelf hardware. Both VL2 [8] and Fat-Tree [1] organize the switches into Clos networks to replace the current practice of multi-rooted-tree-like fabrics. A Clos network is a multi-stage non-blocking network with an odd number of stages [5], and a folded-Clos network is sometimes also called a fat-tree [11]. DCell and BCube [9] propose server-centric topologies to scale a data center with a few added ports on commodity servers. Because of the non-blocking switching capability, Clos networks are promising in data centers and are the focus of this paper.

Given the abundant paths in Clos networks, a desired data center routing scheme should well exploit the paths to improve the system throughput. Randomized routing, which hashes flows (a flow is a stream of packets that have the same values for a subset of fields of the packet header, such as the five-tuple) randomly across network paths, is adopted to achieve load balance in VL2 [8] and Fat-Tree [1]. However, with typical communication patterns, randomized routing design cannot exploit full bandwidth provided by Clos topologies. First, local uncoordinated randomized decisions do not take into account potential flow collisions and traffic unevenness in the network, thus cause unnecessary congestion and reduce the system throughput. Second, the presence of switch failures, which are common for commodity off-the-shelf hardware, may also cause traffic unevenness when fault-agnostic randomized routing is adopted.

To address this problem, in this paper we study alternative routing schemes in data center Clos networks. Clos networks have been used for a long time in the context of High Performance Computing systems (HPCs); routing schemes in Clos networks also have been extensively studied in system area [7,10]. This paper strives to exploit the evaluate the performance and cost of both randomized routing and its alternatives in the context of new data center Clos fabrics. To our best knowledge, routing scheme comparison in data center Clos networks has never been fully exploited before. Hedera [2] is the most related work; it discuss dynamic flow scheduling in Fat-Tree. While our paper discuss the general principals of routings in all Clos networks, especially focus on VL2. Our analysis (Sect. 2) and evaluation (Sect. 6) shows that, in terms of routing, VL2 is much more promising compared with Fat-Tree.

The main contributions of this paper include:

- As an incremental improvement, periodic path renewal is discussed first, where flows are periodically re-hashed to other paths to prevent persistent congestion.
- We bring forward adaptive routing and discuss the question of how to design adaptive routing to fit new Clos fabrics, together with its implementation consideration and costs.
- To combine the merits of both routing schemes and reduce overhead of pure adaptive routing, we further discuss a mixed routing scheme based on flow differentiation.

– We conduct extensive evaluations to these routing schemes. The simulation results show that adaptive routing can better utilize available link bandwidth compared with randomized routing; under the presence of network faults, adaptive routing can "smooth" the network traffic and provides significant higher throughput. While periodic path renewal can provide throughput improvement for randomized routing, its benefit over adaptive routing is almost negligible. The usage of flow-differentiation can significantly reduce the unnecessary overhead of pure adaptive routing without degrading the system throughput.

The rest of this paper is organized as follows. We provide the background of data center traffics and discuss new data center Clos networks in Sect. 2, together with their existing randomized routing designs. We discuss the integration of periodic path renewal technique and comparison between two representative Clos fabrics in Sect. 3. In Sect. 4, we discuss the design, implementation and costs of adaptive routing. Via flow-differentiation, mixed routing reduces the unnecessary overheads of pure adaptive routing, in Sect. 5. We evaluate these routing schemes by extensive simulations in Sect. 6. Related works are provided in Sect. 7. The paper is concluded in Sect. 8.

2   Background

2.1   Traffic Characteristics in Data Center

A highly utilized data mining cluster is instrumented by Greenberg et al. to understand the nature of the traffic matrix of the state-of-art data centers [8]. They got some important data center network measurement results:

Simpler Flow Size: Almost 99 % of flows are myriad small flows (mice), which is smaller than a threshold (100 MB in their cluster). On the other hand, more than 90 % of bytes are carried in flows larger than the threshold (elephants). Compared with Internet flows, the distribution is simpler and more uniform.

Volatile and Unstable Traffic Patterns: The number of representative traffic matrices in data centers is quite large. Also traffic is hard to be predicted, as only 1 % of the time does the network keep the same matrix for over 800 s [8].

Failure is Common: Most failures are small in size while their downtime can be significant. Even conventional 1+1 redundancy are still insufficient, as it is found that in 0.3 % of failures, all redundant components in a network device group became unavailable [8].

2.2   Data Center Clos Networks

Shown in Fig. 1, there are three levels of switches in VL2: ToR (Top of Rack) level, Aggregation level and Intermediate level. As a folded Clos topology [6], VL2 has extensive path diversity. The default routing design in VL2 is randomized:

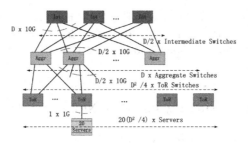

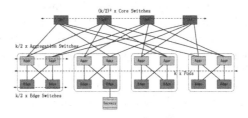

Fig. 1. VL2 Topology [8]

Fig. 2. Fat-tree Topology [1]

a flow from source server takes a random path across source ToR, up to one of two Aggregation switches, via a random chosen Intermediate switch, down to one of two Aggregation switches, across destination ToR, finally reach the destination server. Flow is the basic unit of traffic spreading and thus avoids out-of-order delivery [8].

For this randomized routing, VL2 implements two mechanisms: Valiant Load Balancing (VLB) distributes traffic randomly across intermediate nodes; Equal Cost Multipath (ECMP) makes Intermediate switch failures transparent to servers. VL2 defines anycast addresses for ECMP, each associates with a group of Intermediate switches. The source servers first hash across the anycast addresses; ECMP will then deliver the flows to one of the anycast address's active Intermediate switch.

Shown in Fig. 2, Fat-Tree [1] is also an instance of Clos networks. Edge and Aggregation switches are organized into Pods; Pods are interconnected via Core switches. Fat-tree also presents a randomized routing technique: Edge and Aggregation switches act as traffic diffusers. When faults are observed, a Core switch notifies its neighbors by broadcasting. The neighbors mark the affected link as unavailable and locally choose another link; the Core switch must back propagate the fault information all the way to the endpoints (source) so that subsequent messages exclude routes with the faulty path.

2.3   VL2 v.s. Fat-Tree

Over all, VL2 fabric is more promising from the routing congestion perspective. All links of Fat-Tree are homogeneous, say, 1 GBps. The congestion opportunities could be homogeneous in every layer. For VL2, the links of aggregation layer have 10 times bandwidth than those of access layer. This aggregation effect can significantly alleviate the congestion opportunity. Our evaluations in Sect. 6 confirm the statement.

3   Randomized Routing in Clos Networks

3.1   Drawbacks of Randomized Routing

Randomized routing can achieve load balance and is simple for implementation, where each source locally selects a random middle-stage switch for a flow. However, it can't maximize the system throughput. Local decisions of randomized routing do not take into account potential flow collisions: randomization has the chance that large flows will be hashed to the same links or Intermediate/Core switches respectively, causing unnecessary congestion [8].

Yet another problem is: the presence of faults may cause unevenness in the network traffic when fault-agnostic randomization routing is adopted. For example, if a VL2 Intermediate switch fails in an anycast address group, all flows to this address are undertaken by remaining active switches in the same group. As a consequence, more flows are allocated to active switches in the same group than that of other switches in different groups, and these switches are more likely to be congested. The same situation also happens to a k–ary Fat-tree when a link from an Aggregation switch to a Core switch fails: all traffic are routed to remaining $k/2 - 1$ links of the Aggregation switch. Enlarge the group (e.g. upgrade ECMP to support more ways in VL2), if applicable, would only alleviate this problem, but can't get rid of it.

3.2   Periodic Path Renewal

To prevent persistent congestion, periodic path renewal is a promising technique: each running flow in the network periodically re-hashes its path after a fixed time interval T_r has passed since the last path decision. If large flows are hashed to the same path, they will compete for the path only for a short time and finally some of them will re-hash to other paths. In the presence of traffic unevenness, flows hashed to heavy switches/links are more likely to experience congestion; when their renewal timers time out, those flows have a chance to be hashed out to light switches/links; flows previous in the light ones also have an equal chance to be hashed into heavy ones.

Generally elephant flows could survive at least several renewal periods, especially under heavy network traffic. From a statistical point of view, flows would be equally treated if they persist long enough. We expect that, if periodic path renewal is introduced in, randomized routing can be more fair for flow allocation hence the throughput can be improved.

However, there are still two problems.

- Without a global view of network status, blindly re-hashing flows is not optimal: a flow previously in a contended path may be randomized to another contended or even more contended path; even worse, an elephant in an uncontended path may be unnecessarily randomized to a contended path. These situations would still cause unnecessary congestion and lower the whole throughput.
- In the presence of network faults, local uncoordinated flow allocation is still unfair: some switches/links are been allocated more flows than others. This also results in a degradation of the throughput.

These problems are inherent to randomized routing and are unsolvable by periodic path renewal. For comparison purpose, we also evaluate the effects of periodic path renewal for adaptive routing in Sect. 6.

4   Exploring Adaptive Routing

The idea of adaptive routing is to dynamically find a best path for each flow based on the present network traffic status. Efficient adaptive routing can minimize flow collision that occurs when many flows compete for bandwidth. Adaptive routing is also inherent fault-tolerant to already happened faults: all failed nodes/links are automatically detected/avoided by the routing mechanisms; hence adaptive routing can "smooth out" any unevenness in the network to load balance the traffic to the set of available forwarding switches/links.

For each flow, an adaptive path selection process should be performed first: additional start up delay may be added. Fortunately, such delay can be avoided [9]: when a source is performing path selection for a flow, it does not hold packets. The source uses a default path selecting (e.g. a randomized one) for that flow first. After the routing process completes and a better path is selected, the source switches the flow to the new path.

However, these merits do not come at no cost. The design and implementation of adaptive routing mechanism, either centralized path scheduling or distributed path probing, should be provided. The next two parts present our considerations.

4.1   Centralized Path Scheduling

Centralized path scheduling requires a global view of the network status, including links/ports utilization and nodes health. We expect that a dedicated Fabric Master system periodically receives link utilization reports from switches that take part in forwarding. Routing Agents, either on the application servers or edge switches, would implement the adaptive routing mechanism for flows. We also expect a centralized Routing Scheduler: a Routing Agent sends routing requests for flows to Routing Scheduler; Routing Scheduler replies with the best path back to the sender in a timely manner.

It is assumed that Routing Scheduler use a simple scheduling algorithm to sequentially serve incoming routing requests: (1) finds all available paths between two hosts; (2) selects a best suitable path for the flow.

An illustrative implementation framework is shown in Fig. 3. To avoid single-point-of-failure, both Fabric Master and Routing Scheduler should have replications.

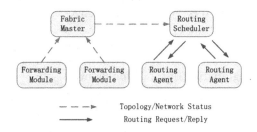

Fig. 3. The Framework of Centralized Path Scheduling

The Fabric Master has a logical matrix with per-link utilization/connectivity information for the entire topology and updates it with the new information. Reports could also serve as heartbeats, which can be used to deduce node/link failure status. Switches can judge its links failure; upon not receiving a report for some configurable period of time, the Fabric Master assumes a switch failure. Fabric Master can be integrated into the existing network control system and should export query interfaces to Routing Scheduler.

Routing Scheduler can be integrated into the existing directory systems in data center Clos network designs [8]: Routing Agent could send lookup requests for each flow which need to perform adaptive routing; after scheduling, the directory system returns the selected routing path information to routing agents as part of the address lookup results. Routing Agents can be integrated into existing Clos networks agents on the application servers (e.g. VL2) or edge switches (e.g. Fat-Tree).

The main cost comes from the mechanism of centralized network status collection. In VL2 topology, Aggregation switches connect both Intermediate switches and ToR switches, hence link utilization reports can be collected solely from Aggregation switches. For a D-port VL2 fabric, there are D Aggregation switches, each with D-port. Each switch port has two directions: *in* and *out*. If we denote utilization of each direction with 1 byte, then an Aggregation switch reports contain $2 * D$ bytes data. That means even a $D = 144$ port switch can report its status in a single packet. If each switch sends reports at a T_r interval, then the number of all report packets is only $1/T_r$ per seconds per switch. Even if each packet is 500 bytes alone, the report only consumes $500*8*1/T_r = 4/T_r$ kbps of each 10G switch. For the whole $D = 144$ fabric (over 100,000 servers), it consumes $4/T_r * 144 = 576/T_r$ kbps. Even if $T_r = 0.1$ s, the network cost is only several Mbps. Calculation of Fat-Tree also gets similar results.

4.2   Distributed Path Probing

The concept of distributed path probing is similar with other literatures [9]: when a new flow came, the source sends probe packets over multiple paths; the passing switches process the probe packets to fill the minimum available bandwidth of their incoming and outgoing links; the destination returns probe responses to the source. When the source receives the probe responses, it selects the best path from them. For simplicity, here we use Broadest Fit (BF) algorithm to select one from available paths: flow is assigned to the broadest path that can provide the maximum bandwidth.

One advantage of data center Clos networks is that all available paths can be easily identified. We take VL2 as an example. Observed that each ToR switch has only two outlet connections, for a pair of source and destination servers there are only $2 * 2 = 4$ possible $\langle source\ Aggregation,\ destination\ Aggregation \rangle$ pairs. With $D/2$ Intermediate switches in a D-port VL2 fabric, there are totally $4 * D/2 = 2 * D$ paths available. Similarly, there are totally $k^2/2$ paths available in a $k-$ary Fat-Tree network. It is apparent that the computation complexity of Broadest Fit routing algorithm is a constant time, which is linear to the network size. That means we can probe all available paths in data center Clos networks, which is almost impossible in hypercube networks [9].

The main cost comes from probing request and response which are proportional to the number of flows. For each request, there are $2 * D$ probing messages for a VL2 network; although the traffic volume is negligible, these path selection mechanism consumes CPU cycle and memory in hosts and network devices. We will evaluate these overheads in Sect. 6. However if mixed routing scheme is adopted (which will be presented later in Sect. 5), this cost can be greatly reduced.

5   Mixed Routing

It is obvious that there is no need to do adaptive routing for *EVERY* flow. As mentioned above in Sect. 2, almost 99 % of flows are less than 100 MB. Compared with elephants, the afforded overhead of traffic engineering to mice may be unnecessary. For example, keep alive operation may has only one or two messages per connection; it is unreasonable to do adaptive routing for such flows.

A mixed routing scheme to control adaptive routing cost can be used by *Flow Differentiation*: mixed routing uses different routing schemes for flows based on its predicted size. To be more specific, we can only perform adaptive routing for elephants and use randomized routing for mice.

Similar load-sensitive routing has been previously proposed in IP routing context [12], while our paper is the first work which evaluates Flow-Differentiation-Based routing in data center networks.

For design consideration, we propose to put the flow differentiation intelligence in the physical servers. Unlike Internet, servers in a data center are controllable.

The next problem of flow differentiation is: how can we identify elephant flows? The answer is to match the flow characteristics with identified patterns definitions. The patterns can be either proactive defined by a system administrator, such as known TCP ports of GFS chunk copy operations. Or, we can reactively change the flow type: all new flows are mice first; after transmitting a certain size, a new flow becomes an elephant flow.

6   Performance Evaluation

6.1   Evaluation Methodology

Topology. We have implemented all algorithms in a flow-level simulator; the TCP AIMD behavior is assumed for flows as that in [2]. The main experiment topology is a full $D = 16$-port VL2 Clos network. The topology has 8 Intermediate switches and 16 Aggregation switches which has sixteen 10 Gigabit ports. There are 64 ToR switches equipped with two 10 Gigabit uplink ports and twenty 1 Gigabit ports to servers. All $N = 1,280$ servers have 1 Gigabit port each. There are two anycast groups in the topology: Intermediate switches from 0 to 3 are assigned to group 0; Intermediate switches from 4 to 7 are assigned to group 1. The Fat-Tree topology is set to $k = 16$ and has 1,024 servers; this topology is only used in Part B for comparison.

Traffic Pattern. The flow size distribution exactly follows the measurement results of a data center [8]. For totally N servers in the network, there are N elephants with size over 100 MB and $99 * N$ mice with smaller size.

We use Paired All-to-All data shuffling pattern [7], as its name suggests, N servers are randomly split to $N/2$ pairs such as that no server is in more than a single pair. Each server is exactly the source of one elephant flow and the destination of one elephant flow. All mice flows are evenly distributed among a period with their source and destination randomly chosen. Elephants patterns and mice together emulate the typical ON-OFF burst communication style in data centers.

Note that we target "medium high load" regime: previous measurement shows that averagely only one large flow per server, and the 75th percentile is 2 [3]; our setting has 2 large flows for every server, which is slightly higher in load than normal scenarios. Our preliminary simulation shows that: when the load is too small in scale, naive random routing is already good enough; also, when the load is too high, there are too many elephant flows in the system, and there is seldom the luxury to improve the throughput by any scheduling scheme.

Metrics. The evaluation metrics include:

– *Maximum Bandwidth Utilization:* This metric reflects the normalized concurrent bisectional bandwidth in the network in percentage. The closer the metric to 100 %, the better a routing scheme utilizes the high capacity provided by the Clos networks. The Maximum Bandwidth Utilization reports the highest utilization during the whole experiment.
– *Elephants (Completion) Delay:* This metric reflects the average normalized completion time of elephants. Assume a minimum elephant flow with size 100 MB, its transmission would be completed in $100\,MB * 8/1\,Gbps = 0.8\,s$ if no congestion occurs; if it is completed in 1 s in an experiment, we denote its normalized completion time as $1/0.8 = 112.5\,\%$. Average completion time is inversely proportional to the achieved throughput of elephants. Generally speaking, the lower the metric, the higher the average elephants throughput.

Table 1. Experiments Scenarios

Scenario	Fail mode	Capacity loss
0	No Fail	0
1	Intermediate 0 Fail	12.5 %
2	Intermediate 0 and 2 Fail	25 %

- *Ratio of Been Selected (Switch):* We use a counter for each Intermediate switch to record how many times it has been selected for flows as the bounce off point. After an experiment, counts of every switch are normalized to their summation. Comparison of these ratios illustrates routing protocols' performance of local uncoordinated flow allocation fairness among switches, especially at the presence of nodes failures.
- *Number of Routing Requests:* This metric reflects the adaptive routing request/response issued throughout the whole data shuffling process. The lower the number, the lower the overhead of adaptive routing schemes.

Failure Scenarios. Throughout this Section, we use three different scenarios, see Table 1. Scenario 0 is ideal where no Intermediate switch fails; scenario 1, to simulate common fail situation, has one Intermediate switch broken; scenario 2 simulates the disastrous situation that broken switches are close in topology (e.g. Intermediate switch 0 and 2 reside in same group in our case). We focus on the Intermediate switches cases because they have direct impact over bisectional throughput.

Protocol Setting. We use *Random* or simply *R* to denote random routing protocol, *Adaptive* or simply *A* to denote pure adaptive routing protocol and *Mixed* or simply *M* for Mixed routing; *Random(NP)* denotes that periodic path renewal is NOT included and so is the others. For simplicity, the renew period is set to 0.1 s for all scenarios.

Centralized Path Scheduling is assumed in the simulation for adaptive routing. In this paper, we limit ourself to evaluate the effect of flow-differentiation performance to mixed routing. We suppose there are a fixed percentage of elephants are misjudged as mice and vice visa; by varying the percentages, we evaluate their effect over routing performance.

6.2 Randomized Routing in VL2 and Fat-Tree

In this part, we compare the performance of randomized routing in VL2 and Fat-Tree. All elephants are injected into the network within 0.4 s: as the minimum elephant needs at least 0.8 s to be transmitted, we can guarantee that all N elephants could compete in the network for at least 0.4 s. All mice are evenly distributed among 10 s. These traffic setting is consistent with the typical ON-OFF type of data center network [8].

Figure 4 presents the comparison of maximum system throughput. Due to the excessive congestion, randomized routing in Fat-Tree can only exploit around

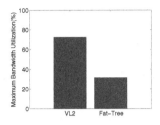

Fig. 4. VL2 v.s. Fat-Tree: Maximum Bandwidth Utilization (%)

30 % network bandwidth. This result is consistent with the Hedera project [2], which is a dedicated work for Fat-Tree traffic engineering. As a comparison, randomized routing can exploit over 70 % available bandwidth provided by Clos networks in VL2.

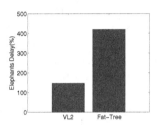

Fig. 5. VL2 v.s. Fat-Tree: Elephants Delay (%)

Figure 5 presents the comparison of average Elephants Completion Delay. Even with periodic path renewal, the *Elephants Delay* of Fat-Tree is around 420 % of standard delay while VL2 is only around 147 % seconds. Obviously the average throughput of VL2 is around 3 times higher than that of Fat-Tree. Due to the superiority of VL2, in later evaluations we will focus on VL2 topology.

6.3   Performance Comparison

In this part, we use scenario 0 (no switch failure) and Paired All-to-All traffic pattern. This experiment can exploit the ability of bandwidth utilization of routing schemes and exemplify the overhead of adaptive routing mechanism. There are 3 routing protocols and the periodic path renewal option, hence together we have 6 schemes to be evaluated.

Figure 6(a) presents the comparison of maximum system throughput. As we have expected, simple randomized routing can only exploit less than 70 % available bandwidth provided by Clos networks; by adding periodic path renewal, the *Random* throughput is only slightly improved to around 72 %. On the contrary, adaptive routing could achieve nearly 90 % maximum bandwidth utilization, i.e. 20 % higher than *Random*. Figure 6(b) also confirms the superiority of adaptive routing: the result of *Adaptive* is close to 110 %; *Random* is around 150 % which implies that average throughput is less than 2/3.

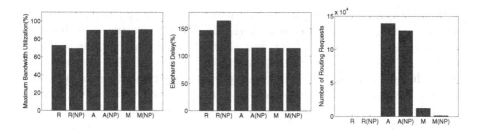

Fig. 6. Paired All-to-All pattern: (a) Maximum Bandwidth Utilization (%) (b) Elephants Delay (%) (c) Number of Routing Requests.

In both Fig. 6(a) and (b), the achieved performance of *Mixed* are almost the same as *Adaptive*. While the Number of Routing Request is significantly reduced by more than 90 %, as shown in Fig. 6(c). We can conclude that the use of flow-differentiation-based routing can significantly reduce the cost of pure adaptive routing while sacrificing minimum performance in ideal traffic pattern.

We can also conclude that, the performance improvement, by adding periodic path renewal, to both *Adaptive* and *Mixed* is almost negligible.

6.4   Resistance to Switch Failure

In this part, we analyze the performance of different schemes under switch failures scenarios.

Figure 7(a) shows simulation results of *Random* randomized routing. When no switch fails, the flows are almost evenly distributed among switches. When Intermediate switch 0 broken down, all flows randomized to anycast group 0 are now shared by other 3 switches. Apparently switches in anycast group 1 are not affected all. Further when Intermediate switch 2 also broken, the numbers of flows allocated to the remaining switches in group 0 (say, 1 and 3) double that allocated to the switches in group 1. It is clear that the presence of faults cause unevenness in the Clos network traffic when fault tolerant randomized routing is adopted.

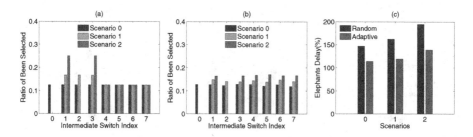

Fig. 7. (a) *Random* Ratio of switch been selected (b) *Adaptive* Ratio of switch been selected (c) Elephant delay comparison under failure.

Figure 7(b) also give the Ratio of Been Selected of *Adaptive* routing. Compared with *Random*, *Adaptive* could fairly distribute flow requests to Intermediate switches under *ALL* failure scenarios: adaptive routing framework can dynamically track the network node status and failed switches are automatically excluded from scheduling; flows are perfectly distributed among all active switches. We can conclude that adaptive routing is particularly useful in local uncoordinated fairness of flow allocation around traffic unevenness caused by the network faults.

Shown in Fig. 7(c), due to capacity loss, Elephants Delay increases for both schemes. Compared with Scenario 0, the performance difference is more apparent in Scenario 1; we even observed over 30 % average throughput improvement of *Adaptive* over *Random* in Scenario 2. It is clear that adaptive routing can "smooth" the traffic unevenness under the presence of network faults. As a result, adaptive routing is free of the risk of unnecessary congestion caused by nonuniformities.

6.5   The Impact of Flow-Differentiation Performance

In this part, we assume that there is a fixed percentage of elephants are misjudged as mice and vice visa; by varying the percentages, we evaluate their effect over routing performance. Two parameters are introduced in:

– *Elephants Error* A fixed percentage of elephants are misjudged as mice.
– *Mice Error* A fixed percentage of mice are misjudged as elephants.

By varying the percentages, we evaluate their effect over routing performance. In this part, *Elephants Error* is increased the from 0 % (perfect judgement) to 30 %, so is the mice.

Figure 8(a) shows that the achieved Maximum Bandwidth Utilizations are almost the same for different scenarios. This is correspondent to the results of Fig. 6(a) and (b): the use of flow-differentiation-based routing sacrifices minimum throughput performance. In Fig. 8(b), Elephants Delay does increase slightly with *Elephants Error*, which suggests that small *Elephants Error* value won't impair the performance of *Mixed* routing.

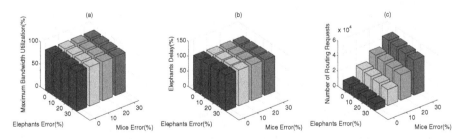

Fig. 8. Impact of Flow-differentiation Performance (a) Maximum Bandwidth Utilization (%) (b)Elephants Delay (%) (c) Number of Routing Requests.

The main difference is shown in Fig. 8(c): the routing overhead increases proportionally with *Mice Error*, which suggests that designers should be careful with their flow differentiation algorithms.

7 Related Work

Research of Clos network is more active in super-computing area: both adaptive routing and randomized oblivious routing have been implemented in a folded-Clos topology. Aydogan et al. showed that an adaptive routing provides better performance than randomized routing on the SP2 network [4]. Kim et al. has a detailed performance analysis and results for adaptive routing in a folded-Clos on chip interconnection, assuming a packet-switched networks [10]. Our research focus on the data center networks which are also packet switching based. The VL2 paper mentioned the possibility of "re-hashing the large flows periodically" to deal with the situations "that large flows will be hashed to the same links and Intermediate switches respectively, causing congestion", also no practical works are presented.

8 Conclusion and Future Work

Through detailed discussions and comprehensive evaluations, we provide data center network designers with useful insights: the usage of flow-differentiation can significantly reduce the unnecessary overhead of pure adaptive routing without degrading the system throughput. Our analysis can be useful to the development of various Cloud service and other networked systems [13–16].

References

1. Al-Fares, M., Loukissas, A., Vahdat, A.: A scalable, commodity data center network architecture. In: ACM SIGCOMM Computer Communication Review, vol. 38, pp. 63–74. ACM (2008)
2. Al-Fares, M., Radhakrishnan, S., Raghavan, B., Huang, N., Vahdat, A.: Hedera: dynamic flow scheduling for data center networks. In: NSDI, vol. 10, pp. 19–19 (2010)
3. Alizadeh, M., Greenberg, A., Maltz, D.A., Padhye, J., Patel, P., Prabhakar, B., Sengupta, S., Sridharan, M.: Data center TCP (DCTCP). ACM SIGCOMM Comput. Commun. Rev. 41(4), 63–74 (2010)
4. Aydogan, Y., Stunkel, C.B., Aykanat, C., Abali, B.: Adaptive source routing in multistage interconnection networks. In: Proceedings of the 10th International Parallel Processing Symposium, 1996, IPPS'96, pp. 258–267. IEEE (1996)
5. Clos, C.: A study of non-blocking switching networks. Bell Syst. Tech. J. 32(2), 406–424 (1953)
6. Dally, W.J., Towles, B.P.: Principles and Practices of Interconnection Networks. Elsevier, San Mateo (2004)

7. Geoffray, P., Hoefler, T.: Adaptive routing strategies for modern high performance networks. In: 16th IEEE Symposium on High Performance Interconnects, 2008, HOTI'08, pp. 165–172. IEEE (2008)

8. Greenberg, A., Hamilton, J.R., Jain, N., Kandula, S., Kim, C., Lahiri, P., Maltz, D.A., Patel, P., Sengupta, S.: VL2: a scalable and flexible data center network. ACM SIGCOMM Comput. Commun. Rev. **39**, 51–62 (2009). ACM

9. Guo, C., Lu, G., Li, D., Wu, H., Zhang, X., Shi, Y., Tian, C., Zhang, Y., Lu, S.: Bcube: a high performance, server-centric network architecture for modular data centers. ACM SIGCOMM Comput. Commun. Rev. **39**(4), 63–74 (2009)

10. Kim, J., Dally, W.J., Dally, J., Abts, D.: Adaptive routing in high-radix clos network. In: SC 2006 Conference, Proceedings of the ACM/IEEE, pp. 7–7. IEEE (2006)

11. Leiserson, C.E.: Fat-trees: universal networks for hardware-efficient supercomputing. IEEE Trans. Comput. **100**(10), 892–901 (1985)

12. Soule, A., Salamatia, K., Taft, N., Emilion, R., Papagiannaki, K.: Flow classification by histograms: or how to go on safari in the internet. ACM SIGMETRICS Perform. Eval. Rev. **32**(1), 49–60 (2004)

13. Tian, C., Alimi, R., Yang, Y.R., Zhang, D.: Shadowstream: performance evaluation as a capability in production internet live streaming networks. In: Proceedings of the ACM SIGCOMM 2012 conference on Applications, Technologies, Architectures, and Protocols for Computer Communication, pp. 347–358. ACM (2012)

14. Tian, C., Jiang, H., Iyengar, A., Liu, X., Wu, Z., Chen, J., Liu, W., Wang, C.: Improving application placement for cluster-based web applications. IEEE Trans. Netw. Service Manage. **8**(2), 104–115 (2011)

15. Tian, C., Jiang, H., Liu, X., Liu, W.: Revisiting dynamic query protocols in unstructured peer-to-peer networks. IEEE Trans. Parallel Distrib. Syst. **23**(1), 160–167 (2012)

16. Tian, C., Jiang, H., Wang, C., Wu, Z., Chen, J., Liu, W.: Neither shortest path nor dominating set: aggregation scheduling by greedy growing tree in multihop wireless sensor networks. IEEE Trans. Veh. Technol. **60**(7), 3462–3472 (2011)

Hierarchical Adaptive Recovery Algorithm in Mobile ALM

Jianqun Cui[1]($\boxtimes$), Wenlin Zhang[1], Feng Huang[1], and Libing Wu[2]

[1] School of Computer, Central China Normal University, Wuhan 430079, China
jqcui@126.com
[2] School of Computer, Wuhan University, Wuhan 430072, China

Abstract. Because of dynamic nature of the application layer multicast node in mobile ALM, the node easily loss. The loss of upper-middle-class multicast tree nodes has a wide range of influence, but the loss of lower nodes, especially the leaf node has a small range of influence. According to this characteristic, Hierarchical Adaptive Recovery (HAR) algorithm is proposed. Firstly HAR stipulates the judging method of core nodes and primary nodes, namely hierarchical method; when the node is missing, based on different nodes loss, it can adopt different recovery strategy to renew the multicast tree. Also it can make the multicast tree more stable and get higher node recovery efficiency. Through the experimental comparison, it is proved that HAR has lower rejoining delay.

Keywords: Mobile ALM · Adaptive recovery · Rejoining delay · Hierarchical method

1 Introduction

The development of application layer multicast technology brings a new direction to the development of streaming media applications in the intelligent terminal. It makes building application layer multicast in a mobile environment to become a hot research topic. Some companies which committed to providing high-definition, smooth professional video services in online video such as Baidu, IQiyi, Youku, etc., have to expand their streaming service to mobile networks [1]. At the same time, Application Layer Multicast [2] as a P2P technology, can reduce the load pressure of streaming media server and optimize the streaming service. So its application in the mobile environment has been a hot topic in recent years.

Intermediate forwarding node of mobile application layer multicast system is a common terminal system as the same as fixed network-based application layer multicast system. Individual node failure or leaves would lead to the multicast tree to split especially the non-leaf node. A non-leaf node leave in multicast tree will affect all nodes which take it as the root node of the sub tree. For example, in a mobile environment, application layer multicast tree is shown in Fig. 1, the leave or failure of user node A will temporarily interrupt the user node D, E, H, I and J receiving the multicast data. Therefore, the affected nodes need to join

© Springer-Verlag Berlin Heidelberg 2015
S. Zhang et al. (Eds.): ICoC 2014, CCIS 502, pp. 95–105, 2015.
DOI: 10.1007/978-3-662-46826-5_8

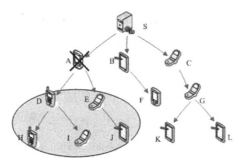

Fig. 1. Splitting graph of multicast tree in mobile environment

the multicast tree again. How to quickly restore the multicast tree to make the affected nodes to receive multicast data as soon as possible is directly related to the quality of the user access to multicast service.

The paper is structured as follows. Section 2 provides an overview of related work. Section 3 proposes a hierarchical adaptive recovery algorithm which divides the mobile environment application layer multicast nodes into two layers. It describes the hierarchical method and the algorithm of each layer multicast nodes redirection strategy in detail. The performance of the algorithm is verified by the simulation in Sect. 4. Finally, we present our main conclusions and future work in Sect. 5.

2   Related Work

The study of stability of application layer multicast in fixed network has two directions. One is to evaluate the performance of terminal nodes [3–5], to calculate the nodes leave probability, and when the node leaves, adjusting the topological structure of children to reduce the risk of the multicast tree. The other one is to make sure children nodes rejoin the multicast tree again as soon as possible by redirecting strategy when a node leaves. The recovery strategy can be divided into active and passive recovery.

Research on stability of application layer multicast of mobile environment is based on that of the fixed network. The references [6,7] represent the passive recovery scheme. When a node leaves, affected nodes of sub tree will be looking for the new father node to rejoin. The references [8,9] adopt establishing redundant virtual link method. This kind of strategy immediately enables the backup path to transmit multicast data to nodes affected when the node leaves. But this scheme is mainly aimed at the network level multicast fault. The references [10,11] provide the emergency parent node in the process of building multicast tree. Once a node leaves, children nodes affected will directly send reconnection news to the emergency parent node, which is a kind of active recovery strategy.

Above the multicast tree recovery strategies are just using a method to restore the multicast tree and they also have low efficiency and high rejoining delay. In addition, compared with traditional distributed computing environment based on the fixed network, the wireless of link, terminal mobility, the wireless network bandwidth, and mobile terminal battery capacity constraints all make mobile computing environment to face a greater challenge. Based on the above reasons, the Hierarchical Adaptive Recovery (HAR) algorithm is presented. When the upper level node in a multicast tree is lost, its children nodes affected will rejoin the multicast tree by setting the redundant nodes; when the lower node is lost, its children nodes affected quickly rejoin the multicast tree by searching a new parent node.

3   Hierarchical Adaptive Recovery Algorithm

In the HAR recovery algorithm, first, it must determine the hierarchical strategy of mobile application layer multicast group member. For this reason, the sub tree height and root path definition are given. The calculating formula is given according subtree height and root path to determine the node level. Second, about the redirection of the upper multicast tree node, HAR uses setting redundancy nodes to ensure rapid redirection. At last, HAR algorithm introduces detailed redirection algorithm in the multicast tree nodes at different levels.

3.1   Hierarchical Method

The hierarchical method of HAR algorithm is similar to the hierarchical loss recovery solution (HR) algorithm presented by reference [11] which is as an extension of the existing tree based on ALM protocol and provides lossless ALM service. The HR algorithm divides multicast tree group members into two recovery plane (the plane 1 and plane 2). In order to effectively recover the loss data, the HR algorithm uses a different but related solution. The losses of data in plane 1, HR use a robust and fast recovery strategy. And it uses low load and low recovery latency strategies in plane 2. For the missing data of a node or more members have the characteristics of small recovery diffusion, HR algorithm uses the area constrained multicast forwarding packet recovery strategy. The HAR algorithm divides the mobile application layer multicast group members into two layers according to the problem of children nodes rejoining to the multicast tree when their father node is lost. All nodes in first layer are called the core node and all nodes in the second layer are called primary node. The core node is normally in the upper part of multicast tree, and the primary node is in the lower part.

As we all known, in the multicast tree, if the upper nodes leave, its impact to the multicast tree on the multicast data transmission is larger than the lower node. So the recovery strategy must be fast and stable for the core node. At the same time, for primary node, the recovery strategy must have low rejoining delay latency. As shown in Fig. 2, it is the hierarchical structure of mobile application layer multicast tree.

In Fig. 2(a), shadow nodes 1–6 are core node and other blank nodes are the primary node. Figure 2(b) shows two layers structure: nodes in dotted border are in the core node layer and nodes in solid border are in the primary node layer.

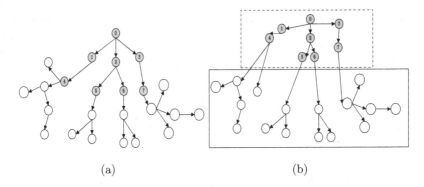

Fig. 2. Hierarchical structure of mobile application layer multicast tree

As you can see from Fig. 2, primary nodes construct the higher level in the tree, while the sub tree height which takes the primary node as root is smaller. Tree level of the core node is relatively lower and the sub tree height which takes the core node as root is larger. According to this characteristic, HAR algorithm uses the following method to divide multicast tree nodes.

In mobile environment application layer multicast tree, each node has a sub tree height. Taking x as the root, sub tree height is $h(x)$, defined as follows:

$$h(x) = \begin{cases} 0 & |Cx| = 0 \\ max|h(c) + 1| \ c \in Cx & otherwise \end{cases} \tag{1}$$

In Eq. (1), Cx is the child nodes set of x and $|Cx|$ is the number of child nodes set. r represents the new joining node, and the sub tree height of new joining node $h(r)$ is 0. m represents the parent node of node r. The algorithm of calculating sub tree height is as follows:

(1) For new joining node r, $h(r) = 0$;
(2) When node r joins the multicast tree, r sends the heightUpdate $(h(r))$ message to its parent node m;
(3) Once node m receives message heightUpdate $(h(r))$ from the child node r, m will do the following:

   If r is the new joining node, m keeps its height value $h(m)$;

   If r isnt the new joining node, then m compares the sub tree heights of all child nodes, and chooses the child node with maximum height $h(max)$. m updates $h(m)$ with $h(max) + 1$;
(4) If node m deletes an existing node, then m recalculates $h(m)$, steps as mentioned above.

In the mobile application layer multicast tree, from the root node to each node, there is a unique loop-free path. All the nodes on the path are called the root path [11]. Using $r(m)$ represents the set of nodes and $|r(m)|$ represents the number of nodes in the collection, the following equation can be used to determine whether the node is the core node or primary node.

$$Chg(m) = \delta(h(m)/|r(m)|) \tag{2}$$

In Eq. (2), δ is configuration parameter to adjust the number ratio of core node and primary node. But in the HAR algorithm, the number of core node and primary node does not affect the superiority of algorithm, so here setting $\delta = 1$.

If $Chg(m) > 1$, the node m is the core node;
If $Chg(m) \leq 1$, the node m is the primary node.

When all nodes join into the multicast tree, it will automatically call $computerChg()$ method to determine level properties.

According to the hierarchical method, HAR can ensure that nodes in the multicast tree top are core node, nodes in the multicast tree lower layer is the primary node.

3.2   Setting Strategy of Redundant Node

Layered multicast tree in HAR algorithm, the recovery of core node is on the basis of redundant node. Redundancy node is that have no child node. Redundant node is set in building multicast tree by selection algorithm.

Selection algorithm of redundant nodes is as follows. When nodes join to the parent node and the parent node has achieved out degree threshold, the parent node determines the load of each child node and selects the lowest load child node as the redundant node. When the core node lost, its children will find the optimal redundant node as its backup parent node.

How many nodes should be set as redundant node is based on the following principle. The redundant node is as new parent node of nodes affected when the core node is lost. So the redundant node is set according to the level of core node. In the simulation experiment, the node out degree threshold is random integer between [2, 4]. If the mobile application layer multicast tree node number is N, then the multicast tree depth is as follows, here height (tree) representing depth:

$$log_4 N < height(tree) < log_2 N \tag{3}$$

So we set the maximum level of redundant nodes is $log_2 N$, when the level of a new joining node is greater than $log_2 N$, the node will not be chosen as the redundant node.

3.3   Core/Primary Node Redirection

1. Core Node Redirection. The specific recovery algorithm steps are as follows:

(1) When a node leaves, it sends DROP_REQUEST message to its father node. And this node also sends DROP_NOTICE message to all the child nodes, notifying the child to find the new father node to rejoin the multicast tree.
(2) When the node receives the DROP_RQUEST message, it will query whether the source node is its child node. If it is, then removes the node, and sends DROP_RESPONSE message back to the source node. If not, deletes the message and do nothing.

(3) When the node receives the DROP_NOTICE message, it will verify whether the parent node is the core node. If it is, then it will take the core node algorithm running steps (4).

(4) The child node affected sends POLL_REQUEST message to its grandfather node to get the new parent address.

(5) When the node receives the POLL_REQUEST message, it verifies whether there is a redundant node. If not, the node will find upper nodes. If the upper layer has no redundant nodes, the node will find lower nodes. When it finds redundant node, it sends POLL_RESPONSE message carrying the parent node back to the source node.

(6) When the node receives the POLL_RESPONSE message, it will get the new father node. Then it will send REJOIN_REQUEST messages to the new parent node to apply to join the multicast tree again.

(7) When the node receives the REJOIN_REQUEST message, if the node has not achieve the out degree threshold, the node is allowed to join, or allowed to join its child node

(8) When all child nodes rejoining are completed, HAR updates node information, including the parent node, level, and tree height.

If the child node is added to the redundant brother of the parent in the best case, the time complexity is $O(1)$. In the worst case, if all redundant nodes reach the out degree threshold, in accordance with the above algorithm, the algorithm has to find until the root node, so the time complexity is $O(log_2 N)$, where N is the level number of loss node.

Pseudo code of redirection algorithm of core nodes is as follows:

Algorithm 1. Redirection Algorithm of Core Nodes

1: // send a redirecting message to the grandfather node;
2: SendMessagetoGrandFather(POLL_REQUEST)
3: //Query redundant node, it will query the nodes in the same level of the loss parent node, then turn to the upper nodes, at last query lower redundant nodes
4: *bool flag = researchReductent()*;
5: **if** (*flag*) **then**
6:     // take the queried node as new father node ;
7:     SendMessagetoNewFather(REJOIN_REQUEST)
8: **end if**
9: // if it is success, then execute 12
10: **if** (complish) **then**
11:     //update the parent node of the nodenode level and the parent tree height.
12:     *UpdateFather()*
13:     *UpdateLevel()*
14:     *UpdateHeight()*
15: **end if**
16: // If any redundant node is not find, the child node directly rejoins the child of grandfather node.
17: *endMessagetoChild(REJOIN_REQUEST)*

The Algorithm of Redirection of Primary Node. The specific recovery algorithm steps are as follows:

(1) When the child node receives a message DROP_NOTICE from loss father node, if the parent node is the primary node, it directly sends REJOIN_REQUEST message to the grandfather node.
(2) When node receives the REJOIN_REQUEST message, if it does not reach the out degree threshold, the node will be allowed to join, otherwise the message is forwarded to the child node.
(3) The child node selection strategy is based on tree height and the number of child node.
(4) When all child nodes rejoining are completed, HAR updates node information, including the parent node, level, and tree height.

Pseudo code of redirection algorithm of core nodes is as follows:

Algorithm 2. Redirection Algorithm of Core Nodes

1: // If the primary node leaves, child nodes add directly to the grandfather node;
2: SendMessagetoGrandfather(REJOIN_REQUEST)
3: // If the grandfather node does not achieve out degree threshold, then it is added directly. Otherwise, select a child node as new parent to rejoin.
4: **if** ($full$) **then**
5:     $researchChild()$;
6:     $SendMessagetoChild()$
7:     //nodes redirection is completed, update node information
8: **end if**

When a node is loss, child node rejoins to the grandfather node. If grandfather node reaches threshold, this node will be added to the suitable child node. So the time complexity is $O(log_2 N)$, where N is the level number of loss node.

4 Experimental Verification and Performance Evaluation

4.1 Simulation Environment

Experiment uses OVERSIM [14] overlay network simulation framework based on OMNET++ [13] network simulation environment to verify the performance of HAR algorithm. Software versions are OMNET++ 4.1, OVERSIM 20101103, and INET 20101019. The hardware environment is the Intel G630C processor, memory for 4 GB. And Operating system is 32 bit Windows 7.

4.2 Experimental Parameters

The experimental parameters meet the following conditions:

(1) Using NICE protocol [12] of fault recovery mechanism and the backup parent node mechanism (BFN) [1] of active detection as a comparative experiment.

The NICE protocol mainly adopts the idea of hierarchical cluster nodes, and supports a number of different data forwarding tree. BFN failure recovery algorithm calculates the backup parent node for each node, and when the node is lost, the child node directly redirects to the backup parent node not searching new parent.

(2) The child node number is in [2, 4] (integer) uniform distribution in the process of constructing the tree.

(3) The leaving probability of all intermediate nodes is set as 20 % to simulate highly dynamic mobile environment.

(4) After all the child nodes complete redirection, a new multicast node left is allowed.

(5) The bottom network is using InetUnderlayNetwork to simulate the mobile environment. As shown in Fig. 3, two backbone routers simulate the two different geographical regions in a mobile environment. In four terminal access routers (overlayAccessRouter), 0–3 represent different mobile base stations in the same region and terminal mobile nodes (overlayTerminal) join a multicast system via a mobile base station to form the overlay network.

4.3   The Delay of Rejoining

Due to the HAR algorithm is based on layered, so here we calculate three kinds of delay which are the core node lost redirection delay, the primary node lost redirection delay and the core and primary node lost redirection delay. The method to count the rejoining delay of node is as follows:

$$Delay = Delay_{end} - Delay_{start} \tag{4}$$

In the Eq. (4), the $Delay_{start}$ represents the start time of father node leaving and the $Delay_{end}$ represents the ending time of child node redirecting new father

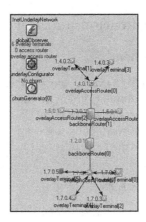

Fig. 3. Simulation architecture diagram of mobile environment

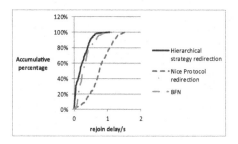 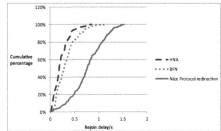

Fig. 4. The accumulative percentage/ rejoining delay of the lost core nodes

Fig. 5. The lost edge nodes accumulative percentage/rejoining delay

node. The total number of nodes used in experiment is 500 and the number of leaving node is 100. The vertical axis represents the percentage of the number of completed redirection nodes and the horizontal axis represents the delay of redirecting time.

Figure 4 shows the delay of the child nodes rejoining multicast tree after core node is lost. From Fig. 4, when the core node is lost, rejoining delay is much smaller than that of NICE protocol, even if both of them adopt passive detection mechanism. The reason is that the failure recovery strategy of core node in HAR algorithm is to look for recent redundant node and has small time complexity. At the same time, the redirection delay of core node is less than BFN algorithm. The reason is that if the backup father node has achieve the out degree threshold, the efficiency of searching new parent is as same as redirection without backup father nodes shown in the reference [1], which has higher time delay by using flooding method.

Figure 5 shows the delay of the child node rejoining multicast tree after primary node is lost. From Fig. 5, we can see the rejoining delay is smaller than NICE protocol and BFN. The reason is that the primary node is node which is in lower layer of multicast tree. When the child node rejoins the multicast tree, the range of looking for new parent node is small, and the time complexity is small.

Figure 6 shows the delay of child node rejoining multicast tree after father node is lost including core node and primary node. From Fig. 6, we can see the rejoining delay with HAR algorithm is smaller than that of NICE protocol and BFN. From Figs. 4 and 5, we can see the rejoining delay of core node and primary node is smaller than that of NICE and BFN.

We count and verify whether the rejoining delay is related to multicast scale (loss nodes numbers). Figure 7 is the average node redirection time delay under different multicast scales. The experimental statistical multicast scales are 10, 20, 30, 40, 50, 60, 70, 80, 90, and 100. In Fig. 7, horizontal axis represents multicast scale, vertical axis represents the average rejoining delay, and the unit is seconds.

From Fig. 7, we can see that the average rejoining delay of HAR is lower than that of NICE and BFN mechanism under different multicast scales. And in different multicast scales, the average rejoining delay of HAR algorithm is

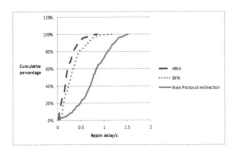
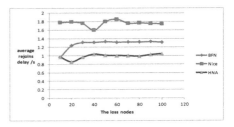

Fig. 6. Lost all of the node percentage/ rejoining delay

Fig. 7. Average rejoining delay/ multi-cast scales

maintained the same. When the multicast scales are 20, because of the number of loss nodes is small, the average rejoining delay of BFN and HAR are same. But as the increasing continuously multicast scale, the rejoining delay of BFN is increasing. From the lengthways, we can see the average rejoining delay of NICE agreement is the highest all the time.

5   Conclusions and Future Work

Based on the performance of different multicast tree nodes, they are divided into core node and primary node according to the sub tree height and root path. When a node leaves, nodes at different levels use different redirection method to perform child node rejoining. And the simulation results demonstrate the effectiveness of HAR. Compared with the two redirection algorithms, BFN and NICE protocol redirection algorithm, HAR shows the optimum rejoining delay. However, there still are many parts need to be improved. For example, primary node can reduce rejoining delay through using bottom-up strategy or other strategies to look for a new parent node. And the low direction delay of the core node also wastes some resources. In the future, we need to study how to improve the efficiency in reducing the waste of resources and reduce the rejoining delay.

Acknowledgments. This work is supported by the National Natural Science Foundation of China (No. 61170017, 61370108, 61272112).

References

1. Cui, J.-Q., Ye, Y.-J., Gao, K., et al.: A quick redirection strategy based on parent node backup mechanism in mobile ALM environment. Comput. Eng. Sci. **35**(12), 39–44 (2013)
2. Peilong, L., Honghai, Z., Baohua, Z., et al.: Scalable video multicast with adaptive modulation and coding in broadband wireless data systems. IEEE/ACM Trans. Networking **20**(1), 57–68 (2012)

3. Hsu, C.-H., Hefeeda, M.: A framework for cross-layer optimization of video streaming in wireless networks. ACM Trans. Multimedia Comput. Commun. Appl. **7**(1), 5 (2011)
4. Cao, J.J., Su, J.S.: Delay-Bounded and high stability spanning tree algorithm for application layer multicast. J. Softw. **21**(12), 3151–3164 (2010)
5. Sripanidkulchai, K., Ganjam, A., Maggs, B., Zhang, H.: The feasibility of supporting large-scale live streaming applications with dynamic application end-points. In: Proceeding of the ACM SIGCOMM, 34(4), pp. 107–120, ACM Press, New York (2004)
6. Zeng, B., Zhang, D., Li, W., et al.: Application layer multicast algorithm based on peer performance evaluation. Comput. Eng. **08**, 13–16 (2009)
7. Peleg, A.: MMX technology extension to the Intel architecture. IEEE Micro. **16**(4), 10–20 (1996)
8. Tremblay, M., O'Connor, J.M., Narayanan, V., et al.: VIS speeds new media processing. IEEE Micro. **16**(4), 10–20 (1996)
9. Moreno, J.H., Zyuban, V., Shvadron, U., et al.: An innovative low-power high-performance programmable signal processor for digital communications. IBM J. Res. Dev. **47**(2.3), 299–326 (2003)
10. Derby, J.H., Montoye, R.K., Moreira, J.: VICTORIA: VMX indirect compute technology oriented towards in-line acceleration. In: Proceedings of the 3rd Conference on Computing Frontiers, pp. 303–312, ACM (2006)
11. Zhang, X.C., Yang, M.H., Zhu, X.J., et al.: A loss recovery approach for reliable application layer multicast. J. Syst. Softw. **85**(5), 1198–1204 (2012)
12. Banerjee, S., Bhattacharjee, B., Kommareddy, C.: Scalable application layer multicast. ACM SIGCOMM Comput. Commun. Rev. **32**(4), 205–217 (2002)
13. Pongor, G.: Omnet: Objective modular network testbed. In: Proceedings of the International Workshop on Modeling, Analysis, and Simulation On Computer and Telecommunication Systems, pp. 323–326, Society for Computer Simulation International (1993)
14. Baumgart, I., Heep, B., Krause, S.: OverSim: a flexible overlay network simulation framework. In: 2007 IEEE Global Internet Symposium, pp. 79–84. IEEE, Piscataway, 11 May 2007

Multicast Storage and Forwarding Method for Distributed Router

Yubao Liu and Wenlong Chen$^{(\boxtimes)}$

Information Engineering College, Capital Normal University,
W.3rd North 56, Haidian 100048, Beijing, China
yubaoliu86@gmail.com, wenlongchen@sina.com

Abstract. With the emergence of Distributed Router, a novel multicast forwarding method called NSFA (Novel Storage and Forwarding Approach) is proposed as the original forwarding approach TSFA (Traditional Storage and Forwarding Approach) has been out of date. In NSFA a new forwarding table model is developed, and what determines the times that packets are switched in the Internal High Speed Switched Networks is the number of outgoing line cards instead of the number of outgoing interfaces. In NSFA, compared with the previous method, the total number of times that packets are switched is considerable lower, which is validated in experiment. Through comparing NSFA and TSFA, it can be found that the memory consumption of NSFA is considerably less than TSFA.

Keywords: Multicast router · Distributed router · Storage and forwarding · Multicast forwarding table

1   Introduction

By the end of 2012, there had been already more than 2400 million [1] Internet users. The popularity of mobile terminals contributed mostly to the increase. Currently, there are about 1500 million mobile device users, while only 100 million last year [1]. At the same time, there occur more and more applications, the datagrams of which have to be sent out from one source to many other endpoints, such as video on demand, IPTV, software updates, interactive conferencing, video conferencing, telemedicine, distance learning, and press releases. With the sharp increase in the number of network users and the wide application of multimedia communications, more and more businesses need to support multicast. Deering of Stanford University first proposed the concept of IP multicasting in his doctoral thesis in 1988 [2–5], and IP multicast was first standardized in 1986 [4], and its specifications have been augmented in RFC 4604 [6] and RFC 5771 [7]. Since 1992, in order to meet the requirements of interactive multicast audio and video businesses, many people committed themselves to studying the

---

Wenlong Chen. Born in 1976, Ph.D., lecturer. His research interests include network protocol, network architecture, high performance router, software defined network.

© Springer-Verlag Berlin Heidelberg 2015
S. Zhang et al. (Eds.): ICoC 2014, CCIS 502, pp. 106–117, 2015.
DOI: 10.1007/978-3-662-46826-5_9

Internet Multicast Backbone (MBONE) [8], which can distribute one packet to many hosts that belong to the same group, but are geographically dispersed.

IP multicast technology is mainly used to solve the problem of efficient multipoint communications [2]. Since the concept of multicast is propounded, it has become a hot topic in the Internet. Without multicast technology, unicast technology would have to be used when the source point, such as your PC, wants to communicate with multiple hosts actively. In this case, the source point, which is called server, has to construct and keep lots of unicast connections with receiving points. The server most likely sends many same data packets to the receiving points, which leads to the waste of network bandwidth. This approach not only increases the load on the server, but also increases unnecessary traffic, and may even cause network congestion.

IP multicast technology enables the transmission to a host group that contains zero or many hosts with the same IP packet. In this technology, the shortest path tree (SPT) [9] or the shared tree (ST) [9] or a combination of both trees is utilized to forward multicast packets. One of the differences between Multicast and Unicast is that the transmission tree is used to switch packets in Multicast, when only one copy of packet needs to be sent, and since then the packet will be copied when needed, often at interactions of the tree. This approach can greatly reduce the amounts of redundant packets, so as to lower the burdens of the server and the Internet to an extraordinary extent. Therefore, Multicast performs better than Unicast in the situation that involves one sender and lots of receivers.

The forwarding table (FT) is fully stored in each line card (LC), a circuit board which can perform the FTs storage and packets forwarding, and the LC has a backup of entire table in scalable Multicast routers in which Multicast technology can be achieved. In this work, a new storage policy is proposed to save memory due to the presence of Reverse Path Forwarding (RPF). At the same instant, the LC number is stored for many times. For example, the outgoing interface list ($OGIL$, one of the entries in Multicast FT) is: $\{1/3, 2/3, 5/3, 7/3, 9/3\}$; in this case the LC number '3' is stored for 5 times, while one is enough in reality. Furthermore, 5 packets are sent to LC_3 (the LC whose LC number equals 3) through the Internal High Speed Switched Networks (IHSN), while one packet is enough in actuality. The redundant forwarding times greatly increase the processing delay and lower the processing performance of routers significantly. In addition, the FT is full backup storage, which wastes lots of memory. Therefore, there are a large number of defects in the traditional storage and forwarding approach (TSFA) and TSFA is not suitable for Distributed Routers. Hence a new policy should be proposed for these routers. In this paper, a novel and more efficient storage and forwarding approach (NSFA) is proposed by cautiously analyzing the shortcomings in TSFA. In this method, only the necessary forwarding entries rather than the whole entries are stored in LC, and it can dramatically lower the switching times (the number of times that a packet is switched) in IHSN. Thereby, NSFA consumes less memory, and the forwarding delay is shorter.

Table 1. Variables and abbreviations

Variables & Abbreviations	Meaning
NSFA	Novel Storage and Forwarding Approach
TSFA	Traditional Storage and Forwarding Approach
MBONE	Internet Multicast Backbone
SPT	shortest path tree
ST	shared tree
FT	forwarding table
FE	forwarding engine
LC	line card
RPF	Reverse Path Forwarding
SR	scalable router
$OGIL$	outgoing interface list
IHSN	Internal High Speed Switched Networks
OF_i	the outgoing interface whose label is i
$OUTLC$	outgoing LC; please refer to Definition 2
$OUTLC_i$	to the outgoing LC whose label is i with respect to $OUTLC$
$OFID$	outgoing interface identification; please refer to Definition 3
LC_{in}	the receiving line card
R_i	the router whose label is i
nlc	total number of line cards
nof	number of outgoing interfaces
nR	total number of scalable routers in Distributed router
$nofp$	the number of outgoing interfaces for a specific multicast packet
$nflc$	the number of forwarding line cards for a specific packet

The rest of the work is organized as follows. In Sect. 2 a novel FT is proposed in NSFA. The forwarding process of multicast packet by means of the new FT model in NSFA is described in detail in Sect. 3. Section 4 is the memory consumption of NSFA, and we make a comparison between NSFA and TSFA. In Sect. 5, the experiment is conducted, and the simulation result is concluded by examining the difference of NSFA and TSFA in the number of switching times in IHSN. Finally, we synchronize and summarize this work in Sect. 6. The variables and abbreviations used in this paper are summarized in Table 1.

2   Design of FT in NSFA

The FT entries of Multicast in TSFA are: $< G, S, IF, FLAG, OGIL >$. G is the multicast group address; S is the source address; IF is the ingoing interface which is the interface by which Multicast packets are received; $OGIL$ is the outgoing interface list. In this paper, new FT entries are proposed in NSFA, which are: $< G, S, IF, FLAG, ROUTER > < OUTLC > < OFID >$. $G, S, IF,$ and $FLAG$ are the same as before, and other parameters are defined as follows.

Definition 1: the definition of $ROUTER$. There may be many scalable routers (SRs) in a Distributed Router as shown in Fig. 1. Assume nR (the number of routers) is the total number of these SRs. All these SRs should be numbered rankly in binary. For example, R_0 can be numbered by '001', R_1 by '010' and R_2 by '100', if the number of SRs is 3.

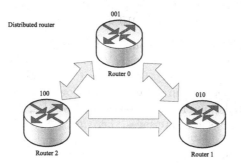

Fig. 1. Distributed router with three SRs

The structure of SRs is shown in Fig. 2 if there are three LCs in one SR. A LC is mainly composed of FT and forwarding engine (FE). There may be many LCs in one SR. To locate LC quickly when forwarding packets, each LC has to be labeled, which will be described in detail in Definitions 2 and 3.

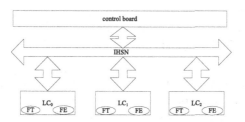

Fig. 2. Structure of SR with three LCs

Definition 2: the definition of $OUTLC$ (outgoing LC). $OUTLC$ denotes the outgoing LC by which packets are sent out, and $OUTLC_i$ refers to the outgoing LC whose label is i. Because the number of LC in each router is usually smaller than 16, here each LC occupies one binary bit. This method will not take too high memory consumption, which will be proved later. If the total amount of LC is nlc (number of LCs), then $OUTLC_i$ ($1 \leq i \leq nlc-1$) is denoted by nlc binary bits ($b_{nlc-1}...b_2b_1b_0$). Here take for example. $OUTLC_0$ (LC_0 is the outgoing LC) is denoted by '001' ($b_0 = 1$), $OUTLC_1$ (LC_1) by '010' ($b_1 = 1$) and $OUTLC_2$ (LC_2) by '100' ($b_2 = 1$), and so on.

Definition 3: the definition of $OFID$ (outgoing interface identification). There are many interfaces in a SR. $OFID$ refers to the outgoing interface (OF), which is used to locate the outgoing interface when forwarding Multicast packets. Let nof (number of outgoing interfaces) denote the total number of outgoing interfaces, and nof binary bits $(b_{nof-1}...b_2b_1b_0)$ are used to denote outgoing interface. Let $OUTID\_LC_j$ ($1 \le j \le nlc - 1$) denote $OGIL$ in LC_j. If $OGIL$ is: $\{0/1, 2/1, 1/2, 3/2\}$, then $OUTID\_LC_1$ is '0101' ($b_0 = b_2 = 1$), the $OUTID$ of LC_1 is '0101' and $OUTID\_LC_2$ is '1010' ($b_1 = b_3 = 1$).

Therefore, the new FT in NSFA is composed of three parts: $< G, S, IF, FLAG, ROUTER >, \{< OUTLC >\}$ and $\{< OFID >\}$. $< OUTLC >$ and $< OFID >$ are included in '$\{\}$'; the meaning of '$\{\}$' is that the total number of those parts is variable, which is depicted in detail in the following example.

If one Distributed Router is composed of three SRs, and each SR has three LCs, and each router has four interfaces, then $nlC = 3$, $nR = 3$, and $nof = 4$. An example is shown in Table 2. Take item 3 for example: $< G, S, IF, FLAG, 111 >$ $< 010 >< 100 >< 101 >< 0111 >< 1110 >< 0001 >< 1110 >$. We know the Multicast packets will be sent to R_0, R_1, and R_3 as $b_0 = 1$, $b_1 = 1$ and $b_2 = 1$ of $ROUTER$ field ('111') which is shown in Stage 1 in Fig. 3.

Table 2. Example of FT

Item	< G, S, IF, FLAG, ROUTER >	< OUTLC >	< OFID >
1	< G1, S1, IF, FLAG, 001 >	< 001 >	< 1000 >
2	< G2, S2, IF, FLAG, 010 >	< 111 >	< 1111 >< 0111 >< 1101 >
3	< G3, S3, IF, FLAG, 111 >	< 010 >< 100 >< 101 >	< 0111 >< 1110 >< 0001 >< 1110 >
4	< G4, S4, IF, FLAG, 011 >	< 100 >< 110 >	< 1011 >< 0011 >< 1100 >
5	< G5, S5, IF, FLAG, 101 >	< 111 >< 100 >	< 0000 >< 1000 >< 1110 >< 1110 >
6	< G6, S6, IF, FLAG, 110 >	< 110 >< 011 >	< 1010 >< 0101 >< 1101 >< 0101 >
7	< G7, S7, IF, FLAG, 011 >	< 100 >< 111 >	< 0010 >< 1110 >< 0111 >< 0110 >

The $OUTLC$ field is: $< 010 >< 100 >< 101 >$; the first one $< 010 >$ is corresponding to R_0, the second one $< 100 >$ to R_1 and the third one $< 101 >$ to R_3. Because the value of $OUTLC$ field is $< 010 >$ with respect to R_0, the packets should be sent to LC_1 ($b_1 = 1$) of R_0 which is shown in Stage two in Fig. 3. Similarly the packets will also be sent to LC_2 of R_1. As the value of $OUTLC$ field of R_2 is $< 101 >$ with respect to R_2, the packets will be sent to LC_0 and LC_2 of R_2 respectively as shown in Stage 2 in Fig. 3.

Next, the $OFID$ field: $< 0111 >< 1110 >< 0001 >< 1110 >$ is explored, and the first one is corresponding to LC_1 in R_0 for $b_1 = 1$ in $< 010 >$ of R_0; the second one is corresponding to LC_2 in R_1 as $b_2 = 1$ in $< 100 >$ of R_1, and the third one and the forth one are corresponding to LC_0, LC_2 respectively in R_3 for $b_0 = 1$ and $b_2 = 1$ in $< 101 >$. Take $< 0111 >$ (the outgoing LC in R_0 is LC_1) for example. OF_i refers to the outgoing interface whose label is i for a specific Multicast packet. The packets will be sent to OF_0, OF_1, and OF_2 respectively as $b_0 = b_1 = b_2 = 1$, which is illustrated in Stage 3 in Fig. 3. Similarly, the packets will be sent to OF_1, OF_2, and OF_3 by means of $< 1110 >$ with respect to LC_2 for $b_1 = b_2 = b_3 = 1$. Both $< 0001 >$ and $< 1110 >$ belong to R_2, $OUTID\_LC_0$ ='0001', $OUTID\_LC_2$ ='1110', and the forwarding sequence is illustrated in Fig. 3. This figure reflects the procedure of looking up FT logically in Distributed Router. Note that the arrows between Stage 2 and Stage 3 do not refer to the actual times that a packet is forwarded in IHSN in Fig. 3. The real forwarding procedure is shown in detail in the next section.

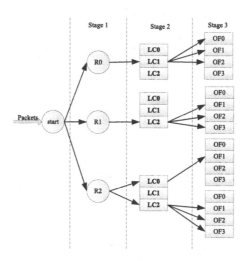

Fig. 3. Packet forwarding components

3   Forwarding Process in NSFA

The FT lookup process can be divided into three stages as indicated in Fig. 3: (1) to locate the router, (2) to locate the LC, and (3) to locate the OF. This method can reduce the switching times dramatically in IHSN. Take Item 2 for example in Table 2: $< G2, S2, IF, FLAG, 010 >< 111 >< 1111 >< 0111 >< 1101 >$. As the value of $OUTLC$ field is $< 111 >$, the packets have to be sent out through LC_0, LC_1, and LC_2. It is easy to find that $OUTID\_LC_0$ ='1111', $OUTID\_LC_1$ ='0111', and $OUTID\_LC_2$ ='1101' in R_2, as the $ROUTER$ field is '010'. The $OGIL$ in TSFA is $\{0/0, 1/0, 2/0, 3/0, 0/1, 1/1, 2/1, 0/2, 2/2, 3/2\}$ with regard to Item 2. The packets have ten copies and are switched for ten times in IHSN, which is conducted in the receiving LC which is denoted by LC_{in} (one LC in LC_0, LC_1, and LC_3) in Fig. 4; meanwhile this approach tends to waste too much bandwidth of IHSN, and increases the processing delay when a packet needs to be forwarded.

In this work, NSFA is proposed to address those problems. Actually only three copies of a packet are needed in NSFA, and the packet only need to be switched for three times in IHSN. Firstly, we know packets will be sent to R_2 by means of $< G2, S2, IF, FLAG, 010 >$ after looking up FT, and then we can perceive that the packet has to be sent to LC_0, LC_1, and LC_2 by $< 111 >$

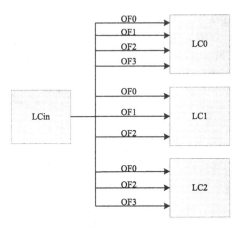

Fig. 4. Switching times in TSFA with respect to Item 2 in Table 2

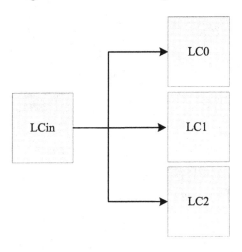

Fig. 5. Switching times in NSFA with respect to Item 2 in Table 2

(the value of $OUTLC$ field). Thereafter, we have recognized $OUTID\_LC_0 =$ '1111', $OUTID\_LC_1 =$ '0111', and $OUTID\_LC_2 =$ '1101' from '< 1110 >< 0111 >< 1101 >'. The LC_{in} must add $OUTID\_LC_0$, $OUTID\_LC_1$, and $OUTID\_LC_2$ to side information of one Multicast packet which should be sent to the corresponding LC respectively. When LC_0 received the information of $OUTID\_LC_0 =$ '1111', it perceives the packet should be sent out through OF_0, OF_1, OF_2, and OF_3, respectively. Therefore, this method largely lowers the switching times in IHSN.

Actually, the switching times in TSFA are only associated with the number of outgoing interfaces of a specific multicast packet ($nofp$) which can be inferred from Fig. 4. The $nofp$ is ten in last example, and then the packet is switched for ten times in IHSN, whereas the switching times in NSFA are only connected with the number of forwarding LC ($nflc$) for a specific packet, which is indicated in Fig. 5. In the last case, the $nflc$ equals three; therefore the packet is switched for three times in IHSN.

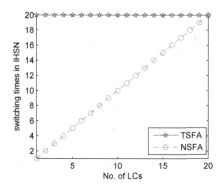

Fig. 6. Switching times with respect to $nflc$

Figure 6 illustrates the variation of switching times with respect to $nflc$ between TSFA and NSFA, when $nofp$ equals 20. TSFA and NSFA have the same switching times only if $nflc$ equals $nofp$ as shown in Fig. 6. In this situation each LC is equipped with only one outgoing interface for a specific Multicast packet, and the switching times amounts to the maximum. It can be indicated that the NSFA can dramatically lower the switching times especially when $nofp$ is much larger than $nflc$.

Each LC has at least one outgoing interface when $nflc$ equals 16 for a specific packet, and then the switching times will not be smaller than 16 as shown in Fig. 7. This figure reveals the variation of switching times with regard to $nofp$. The switching times always equals 16 in NSFA as one LC only needs one copy of packet, whereas it increases steadily in TSFA. We can conclude that the

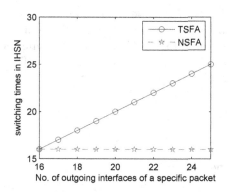

Fig. 7. Switching times with regard to $nofp$

switching times are much larger in TSFA than NSFA when $nofp \gg nflc$, and they are supposed to have the same switching times if $nofp$ equals $nflc$.

4   Storage Analysis in NSFA

The entire of FT in TSFA is $< G, S, IF, FLAG, OGIL >$, and then the memory consumption of each field is denoted by S_g, S_s, S_{if}, S_{flag}, and $(\lceil log_2nof \rceil + \lceil log_2nlc \rceil) * nofp$, respectively. Therefore, the total memory consumption of each FT entre in TSFA is:

$$S_{tsfa} = nlc * (S_g + S_s + S_{if} + S_{flag} + (\lceil log_2nof \rceil + \lceil log_2nlc \rceil) * nofp) \quad (1)$$

Each entire has to be stored in every LC, whereas only part of the FT is stored in NSFA according to the IF field. In NSFA, the entire of FT is $< G, S, IF, FLAG, ROUTER > \{< OUTLC >\} \{< OFID >\}$, and the forwarding process is briefly shown in Fig. 8: (1) to start with one LC_{in} has received a packet, (2) to check group address and source address, (3) to conduct RPF, (4) to forward the packet according to $OFID$ after looking up the FT, and the packet will be discarded if any process does not work [10]. Only the forwarding entries whose IF belongs to the LC are stored in NSFA, as others will not be matched forever. For example, LC_{in} have four interfaces: $\{0/0, 1/0, 2/0, and3/0\}$; the IF forwarding entries should belong to this set as the entries such as $< G, S, 0/1, FLAG >$ and $< G, S, 1/2, FLAG >$ are meaningless and it will not be matched forever. Therefore, the IFs of FT entries do not belong to the set $\{0/0, 1/0, 2/0, and3/0\}$ do not need to be stored, and then the maximum whole memory consumption of each FT entre in NSFA is:

$$S_{nsfa} = S_g + S_s + S_{if} + S_{flag} + (1 + nlc) * nR + nof * nflc \quad (2)$$

If $nlc = 16$, $nof = 16$, $nR = 1$, and $S_g + S_s + S_{if} + S_{flag} = 1$ then

$$S_{tsfa} = 16 * (1 + 8 * nofp) \quad (3)$$

according to expression (1), and

$$S_{nsfa} = 18 + 16 * nflc \quad (4)$$

According to expression(2), the slope equals 128 in TSFA while the slope is 16 in NSFA, which can be inferred from (3) and (4). The memory consumption of TSFA and NSFA is shown in Fig. 9. The memory consumption of NSFA is lower than that of TSFA, and its slope is smaller than that of TSFA. Therefore, NSFA possesses higher memory performance than TSFA.

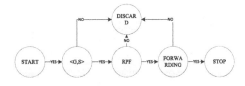

Fig. 8. Forwarding process for each packet

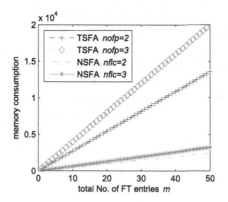

Fig. 9. Memory consumption

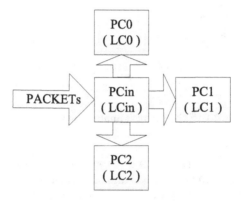

Fig. 10. Scheme of experiment

5 Experimental Analysis

To make comparisons between TSFA and NSFA, assume $nR = 1$ as TSFA is only suitable to one router. Three Linux PCs are used to simulate LC in the router, and PC_{in}, any one of PC_0, PC_1, and PC_2, is corresponding to LC_{in} as shown in Fig. 10. The FT is constructed randomly in PC_{in}. In TSFA the FT is generated by $< G, S, IF, FLAG, OGIL >$, whereas in NSFA the FT is created though $< G, S, IF, FLAG, ROUTER > \{< OUTLC >\} \{< OFID >\}$ like Table 2. The packet will be sent to PC_0, PC_1, or PC_2 by PC_{in} after looking up the corresponding FT.

The experimental algorithm is shown in Table 3, and m packets are generated randomly. Each TSFA packet contains the information of G, S, IF, $FLAG$, $OGIL$, and each NSFA packet consists of the information of G, S, IF, $FLAG$, $ROUTER$, $OUTLC$, $OFID$.

Figure 11 illustrates the relationship between the switching times and the number of forwarding packets while $m = 50$. The times for which packets are

Table 3. Experimental algorithm

Step	Instruction
S1	m multicast packets are produced randomly in PC_{in}
S2	these packets are forwarded after matching the FT, and counters are placed to record the number of forwarding packets
S3	the PCs who received these packets set counters to calculate them

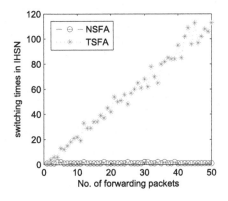

Fig. 11. Experimental analysis when $m = 50$

switched in TSFA rise rapidly from 0 to about 120, whereas the times in NSFA fluctuate smoothly and are not more than three because only three LCs exist in this experiment. Therefore, NSFA can reduce switching times dramatically with the increasing number of multicast packets.

6   Conclusion

In this work, the novel multicast forwarding method NSFA is proposed to fit into the Distributed Router. In NSFA a new FT model is designed, and the whole forwarding information, including the outgoing interfaces in each outgoing LC, can be obtained from it, and the information of outgoing interfaces should be added to the side information of one specific Multicast packet, and then it is supposed to be sent out to the responding outgoing LC. Finally packets will be sent out through the outgoing LCs. By means of this forwarding method (NSFA), the number of times that a packet is switched in IHSN is controlled by the number of outgoing LC, and has nothing to do with the number of outgoing interfaces. The total number of times that the packets are switched in IHSN is largely lower than TSFA, which is verified by experiment. The memory consumption of these two methods is also explored. Though examining the memory consumption of TSFA and NSFA, we can conclude that the performance in NSFA is higher than TSFAs in this regard.

Acknowledgement. Thanks for the instruction of Haiyang Wang, Assistant Professor of Department of Computer Science in University of Minnesota at Duluth, and this research is supported by NSFC Project (61272446, 61373161) and Science &Technology Project of Beijing Municipal Commission of Education, China(KM201420028015).

References

1. Meeker, M.: D11 conference. Internet Trends Report (2013)
2. Deering, S.: Multicast Routing in a Datagram Internetwork. Doctor of Philosophy Ph.D. thesis, Stanford University (1991)
3. Deering, S.E., Cheriton, D.R.: Host Groups: A Multicast Extension tothe Internet Protocol. RFC 966, December 1985
4. Deering, S.E.: Host Extensions for IP Multicasting. RFC 988, July 1986
5. Deering, S.: Host Extensions for IP Multicasting. RFC 112, August 1989
6. Haberman, B.: Using Internet Group Management Protocol Version 3 (IGMPv3) and Multicast Listener Discovery Protocol Version 2 (MLDv2) for Source-Specific Multicast. RFC 4606, August 2006
7. Cotton, M., Vegoda, L., Meyer, D.: ANA Guidelines for IPv4 Multicast Address Assignments. RFC 5771, March 2010
8. Eriksson, H.: MBONE: The multicast backbone. Commun. ACM **37**(8), 54–60 (1994)
9. Estrin, D., et al.: Protocol Independent Multicast-Sparse Mode (PIM-SM): Protocol Specification. RFC 2117, June 1997
10. Parkhunst, W.R.: Cisco Multicast Routing and Switching. McGraw-Hill, New York (1999)

P2P Traffic Identification Using Support Vector Machine and Cuckoo Search Algorithm Combined with Particle Swarm Optimization Algorithm

Zhiwei Ye[(⊠)], Mingwei Wang, Chunzhi Wang, and Hui Xu

School of Computer Science,
Hubei University of Technology, Wuhan, China
weizhiye121@163.com

Abstract. As peer-to-peer (P2P) technology booms lots of problems arise such as rampant piracy, congestion, low quality etc. Thus, accurate identification of P2P traffic makes great sense for efficient network management. As one of the optimal classifiers, support vector machine (SVM) has been successfully used in P2P traffic identification. However, the performance of SVM is largely dependent on its parameters and the traditional tuning methods are inefficient. In the paper, a novel hybrid method to optimize parameters of SVM based on cuckoo search algorithm combined with particle swarm optimization algorithm is proposed. The first stage of the proposed approach is to tune the best parameters for SVM with training data. Subsequently, the SVM configured with the best parameters is employed to identify P2P traffic. In the end, we demonstrate the effectiveness of our approach on-campus traffic traces. Experimental results indicate that the proposed method outperforms SVM based on genetic algorithm, particle swarm optimization algorithm and cuckoo search algorithm.

Keywords: P2P traffic identification · Support vector machine · Cuckoo search algorithm · Particle swarm optimization algorithm

1 Introduction

A peer-to-peer (P2P) system is a self-organizing system of equal, autonomous entities designed for the shared usage of distributed resources in a networked environment without central services [1, 2]. It is popular around the world as a new mode of Internet application, which has been widely used in download, instant message, PPTV, distributed computation and so on. More and more network bandwidth has been occupied by P2P applications, it is estimated that more than 70 % of the whole traffic is P2P in Internet [1]. As P2P technology booms a lot of problems arise, for instance, decentralized networks introduce new security issues as they are designed so that each user is responsible for controlling their data and resources. Moreover, Peer-to-peer networks, along with almost all network systems, are vulnerable to unsecured and unsigned codes that may allow remote access to files on a victim's computer or even compromise the entire network. A user may encounter harmful data by downloading a file that was

© Springer-Verlag Berlin Heidelberg 2015
S. Zhang et al. (Eds.): ICoC 2014, CCIS 502, pp. 118–132, 2015.
DOI: 10.1007/978-3-662-46826-5_10

originally uploaded as a virus disguised in an exe, mp3, or any other file type due to the lack of an administrator maintaining the list of files being distributed. Network security problem has currently become more critical. Trojan horses, worms, DDoS attacks and network abuse can damage network resources and bring inconvenience to the society and people's lives. As a result, it is very important to identify the P2P traffic for the QoS guarantee in the plan and design of network, much effort has been made on this topic, in general, the existing approaches mainly could be divided into following categories [3–15].

(1) Port number based approaches. They are based on TCP/UDP port number. Destination port number of datagram header source is used to identify common traffic. However, with the development of the P2P technology, the accuracy of the technology is gradually decreased, mainly due to the following reasons: (a) camouflage port technology, some P2P applications use the well-known port number of the application (for example, port 80) to camouflage the function port; (b) user-defined port technology, some P2P applications allow users to manually configure the port number, which makes port number no longer fixed; (c) random port technology, some P2P applications using random port allocation technology, making the port number of P2P applications become unpredictable [3, 4].

(2) Signature based approaches. In order to overcome the disadvantages of the above approach, a more trusty technique is to inspect the packet payload. This approach improves the accuracy of traffic identification greatly. Bleul et al. [5] design a simple, effective and flexible P2P flow identification system based on signature-matching in [6]. Young J. Won et al. [7] improve the approach of signature-matching, and prove that signature matches the five packets to the network stream can identify the network traffic. However, some limitations still remain, firstly, most P2P protocols are proprietary and reverse engineering is needed. Secondly, they cannot deal with brand-new applications that use unknown P2P protocols. Thirdly, they are unable to detect P2P traffic encrypted, even when only protocol headers are encrypted. Thus, signature based approaches are no longer suitable for traffic identification.

(3) Traffic behavior based approaches. It uses the information obtained from IP headers. Hence, traffic behavior based approaches could overcome the disadvantages of signature based techniques and port number based techniques. It will not be affected by the payload encryption and can scale high to speed links. But the approach cannot do an accurate classification for P2P traffic due to the approach is only applied to analysis of traffic records, so it is not real time and efficient [8–10].

(4) Machine learning based approaches. In essence, P2P traffic identification is a problem belongs to pattern recognition, which is to classify traffic into P2P and non-P2P. Naturally various classification approaches based on statistical characteristics have been applied to P2P traffic identification [11–15]. For example, Bayesian methods are conducted to identify the P2P traffic in [11, 12], Refs. [12, 13] employed Neural Network to identify P2P traffic. But these methods have some disadvantages, firstly, due to the learning rate is fixed, Neural Network requires a longer training time and the learning and memory ability of neural network are unstable. The prior probability of

Bayesian method is difficult to estimate and the assumption of independence between features is difficult to exist. Support vector machine (SVM) is a powerful machine learning approach for classification and regression problems of small samples and high dimensions, which was initially presented by Vapnik in the last decade of the 20th century based on statistical learning theory and structural risk minimization principle [16]. It has been widely used for security identity and image processing.

However, performance of support vector machine (SVM) is largely dependent on its parameters. In the procedure of classification by SVM, penalty factor C and kernel parameter σ have great effect on the performance of classification. How to get the best parameters is a hot topic in SVM. The common used approaches for tuning the best parameters for SVM are grid search approach, genetic algorithm (GA), particle swarm optimization algorithm (PSO) and so on. However, there are many shortcomings in these approaches. For instance, for grid search approach has to bear a heavy computational burden. GA has poor local search ability and is prone to premature convergence; moreover, it is relatively time-consuming and low efficiency search in the later stage of evolution [17]. PSO has advantages of easy implementation, robustness to control parameters and computation efficiency, and has been successfully applied to optimization problem [18–21]. But it is easy to fall into local optimization. Cuckoo search (CS) algorithm is a newly proposed population based stochastic global search algorithm by Yang [22]. CS can better converge to the optimal solution, but its convergence rate is not well [23]. By using the advantages of CS and PSO, a hybrid optimization algorithm of PSO and CS (shorten to CS_PSO) was proposed by Fan Wang [24]. The algorithm can improve the performance of both Cuckoo search and particle swarm optimization. Hence, in the paper, CS_PSO is proposed to handle with the parameters of SVM and used in P2P traffic identification.

The rest of the paper is organized as follows. Section 2 describes basic principle and relative work of SVM parameter optimization. Section 3 gives a brief description about hybrid Cuckoo Search algorithm and Particle Swarm Optimization algorithm. The proposed CS_PSO based SVM model is detailed in Sect. 4. Section 5 presents the implementation of the proposed model and simulation result. Finally the conclusion is drawn in Sect. 6.

2   The Basic Principle of Support Vector Machines

Support Vector Machines (SVM) is a machine learning approach based on the statistical theory, which could find the optimal solution of the classification results with limited information about a small sample dataset. SVM is able to avoid the shortcomings of many machine learning approaches, such as large sample data sets required, appropriate model established for specific problems [25]. SVM use the idea of kernel function to transform nonlinear problem into linear problem, and reduce the complexity of the algorithm [26]. By kernel transformation and optimization, the optimal problem could be converted into an extremism problem of quadratic convex function. In theory, the approach of SVM is bound to get the global optimal solution.

2.1   The Basic Theory of Support Vector Machines

SVM is development of the optimal surface in condition of linearly separable. The idea can be described by 2 dimensional cases. We can see the optimal hyper-plane as Fig. 1.

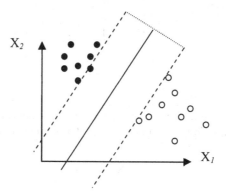

Fig. 1. Representation of hyper planes

In Fig. 1, maximum-margin hyper-plane and margins for an SVM trained with samples from 2 classes. Samples on the margin are called as support vectors [25].

Suppose given some training data D, a set of n points of the form:

$(x_i, y_i), i = 1, 2, \ldots, n, x \in R^n, y \in \{1, -1\}$, where the y_i is either 1 or -1, indicating the class to which the point x_i belongs. Each x_i is a p-dimensional real vector. Hyperplane could be written as (1) [25]:

$$\omega \cdot x - b = 0. \tag{1}$$

If the training data are linearly separable, the general form of the discriminant function can be stated as (2) [25]:

$$f(x) = \omega \cdot x + b \tag{2}$$

Subject to constraints:

$$y_i[(\omega \cdot x_i) + b] - 1 \geqslant 0, i = 1, \ldots, n \tag{3}$$

b is the classification threshold and ω is one-dimensional coefficient vector of the separating hyper-plane in the high-dimensional feature space. Its classification principle can be stated as below [25].

$$\min = \frac{1}{2} \|\omega\|^2 \tag{4}$$

The optimal hyper-plane problem may be converted into convex quadratic programming optimization dual problem. The dual problem may be expressed as (5) [25]:

$$\max \sum_{i=1}^{n} a_i - \frac{1}{2}\sum_{i=1}^{n}\sum_{j=1}^{n} a_i a_j y_i y_j (x_i \cdot x_j) \tag{5}$$

Subject to constraints:

$$a_i \geqslant 0, i = 1, \ldots, n \tag{6}$$

$$\sum_{i=1}^{n} a_i y_i = 0 \tag{7}$$

a_i is Lagrangian multiplier, because the problem is about quadratic function optimization, we can get a unique solution. If a_i^* is the optimal solution, so

$$\omega^* = \sum_{i=1}^{n} a_i^* y_i x_i \tag{8}$$

a_i^* is support vector.

If the training set is not linearly separable, the optimal hyper-plane cannot separate 2 types completely, in order to seek a certain balance between the empirical risk and the promotion of performance, the relaxation factor (ε) is introduced that allows the presence of misclassified samples. By adding the penalty factor (c) in minimizing objective, the objective function can be expressed as (9) [25]:

$$\Phi(\omega, \varepsilon) = \frac{1}{2}\|\omega\|^2 + C\sum_{i=1}^{n} \varepsilon_i \tag{9}$$

Subject to constraints:

$$y_i[(\omega \cdot x_i) + b] \geqslant 1 - \varepsilon_i, i = 1, \ldots, n \tag{10}$$

With $0 < \varepsilon_i < 1$, if the sample points x_i are classify correct; else $\varepsilon_i \geqslant 1$

The optimal hyper-plane problem can be transformed into convex quadratic programming optimization dual problem. The dual problem could be expressed as follows:

$$\max \sum_{i=1}^{n} a_i - \frac{1}{2}\sum_{i=1}^{n}\sum_{j=1}^{n} a_i a_j y_i y_j (x_i \cdot x_j) \tag{11}$$

$$s.t.\, 0 \leqslant x_i \leqslant C, i = 1, \ldots, n \tag{12}$$

$$\sum_{i=1}^{n} a_i y_i = 0 \tag{13}$$

2.2 SVM Parameters Optimization

As there are many non-linear problems in practice SVM utilizes kernel function transform to solve the problem. In 1992, Bernhard E. Boser, Isabelle M. Guyon and Vladimir N. Vapnik suggested a way to create nonlinear classifiers through applying the kernel trick to maximum-margin hyper planes [26]. This permits the algorithm to fit the maximum-margin hyper plane in a transformed feature space. The transformation may be nonlinear and the transformed space may be high dimensional; thus though the classifier is a hyper plane in the high-dimensional feature space, it may be nonlinear in the original input space. Hence, the optimization problem could be represented as below.

$$\max Q(a) = \sum_{i=1}^{n} a_i - \frac{1}{2} \sum_{i=1}^{n} \sum_{j=1}^{n} a_i a_j y_i y_j K(x_i, x_j) \tag{14}$$

The most used Common Kernel functions is RBF kernel function as shown below.

$$K(x_i, x_j) = \exp(\frac{-||x_i - x_j||^2}{\sigma^2}) \tag{15}$$

The parameters σ in kernel function reflect the characteristics of training data and greatly affect the generalization ability of the SVM. Penalty actor c determines the trade-off cost between minimizing the training error and minimizing the model's complexity, whether the value is too big or small will reduce the generalization of SVM. In the paper, the proposed approach aims to optimize the kernel parameters and reduce the number of support vectors efficiently.

3 Hybrid Cuckoo Search and Particle Swarm Optimization

3.1 Overview of Particle Swarm Optimization Algorithm

Particle swarm optimization (PSO) is a population-based stochastic search algorithm first proposed by Kennedy and Eberhart [18] in 1995. PSO has two notable features different from other evolutionary algorithms. Firstly, PSO is a stochastic evolutionary algorithm that does not incorporate survival of the fittest, and all individuals are retained as members of the population through the course of the run. Secondly, there are no conventional evolutionary operators such as crossover and mutation in PSO. It is easy to implement with quick search speed and widely applied to optimization problems that are partially irregular, noisy, change over time, etc. [18–21]. PSO is based on iteration model. In the procedure of optimization, every particle's fitness value is determined by the value of corresponding optimization function. Each particle has two types of information: the particle own flying experience denoted with historical best position of individual particle (p_{id}) and flying experience of particle swarm denoted with historical best position of particle swarm (p_{gd}). Particle and groups cooperate with each other, the relationship between particle movement and group activities are coordinated. Given the population of particles is n, every particle's location is represented as $x_i = (x_{i1}, x_{i2}, \ldots, x_{id})$, particle's speed is $V_i = (v_{i1}, v_{i2}, \ldots, v_{id})$. Particle's velocity and location is adjusted as (16–17).

$$v_{id}(t+1) = \omega v_{id}(t) + c_1 r_1 [p_{id} - x_{id}(t)] + c_2 r_2 [p_{gd} - x_{id}(t)] \tag{16}$$

$$levy(\lambda) \sim u = t^{-\lambda}, 1 < \lambda < 3 \tag{17}$$

In the above expressions, $p_g d$ is historical best position in the whole group, p_{id} is particle's current historical best position, c_1 and c_2 are acceleration constants, commonly set as $c_1 = c_2 = 2$, r_1 and r_2 are random real number drawn from $U(0, 1)$, ω is inertial weight.

3.2   Cuckoo Search Algorithm

Cuckoo search (CS) is an optimization algorithm developed by Xin-she Yang and Suash Deb [22]. It was inspired by the obligate brood parasitism of some cuckoo species which lay their eggs in the nests of other host birds [22]. Some host birds may find these extraneous eggs, these eggs will be discarded or the nest will be abandoned and a new nest will be built elsewhere. CS idealized such breeding behavior and has been applied for various optimization problems. CS is based on three idealized rules: (1) Each cuckoo lays a egg at a time, and dumps it in a randomly selected nest; (2) The optimal nests with high quality of eggs (solutions) will be kept up to the next generation; (3) The number of available host nests is a constant number, and a host can discover an alien egg with a probability $p_a \in [0, 1]$. In this case, the host bird can either throw the egg away or give up the nest and build a completely new nest in a new location [22].

In CS algorithm, each egg in nest represents a solution, and a cuckoo egg denotes a new solution. The goal is to use the new and potentially better solutions to substitute a not so good solution in the nests. Suppose in the D-dimensional space, the nest's position is $X_i = (x_{i1}, x_{i2}, \ldots, x_{id})$, $i = 1, 2, \ldots, n$, local best solution is $p_t = (p_{i1}, p_{i2}, \ldots p_{id})$ and global best solution is $p_g = (p_{g1}, p_{g2}, \ldots p_{gd})$. The nest's position is updated according to following formula.

$$x_i(t+1) = x_i(t) + a \oplus levy(\lambda) \tag{18}$$

$$levy(\lambda) \sim u = t^{-\lambda}, 1 < \lambda < 3 \tag{19}$$

Here a is step size related to the scales of the problem of interest and $a > 0$. In iteration, a new solution is generated from scratch with a certain probability p_a and this solution is inserted in place of the lowest fit solution. This handles the problem of convergence on local optimal solutions efficiently. The pseudo code of CS is as below.

Objective Function $f(x)$, $X = (x_1,...,x_d)^T$

Initialize the population of n host nests x_i

while (t<Max number of iterations)
Get a cuckoo randomly/generate a solution by levy flights
and then evaluate its quality/fitness F_i

  Choose a nest among n(say, j) randomly
if ($F_i > F_j$)

Replace j by the new solution
end
A fraction (p_a) of worse nests are abandoned and new so-
lutions are built
Keep best solutions
Rank the solutions and find the current best
end while
Postprocess results and visualization

3.3   Hybird Cuckoo Search and Particle Swarm Optimization Algorithm

CS_PSO is a hybrid algorithm which combines PSO and CS. It persists in high searching efficiency of PSO and inherits the ability of obtaining high grade solution in the whole searching space. Thus the hybrid algorithm enhances the searching precision and optimizing ability of the primitive methods. The basic thought of CS-PSO is that at an iteration it first carries out PSO to get a group of optimal positions, then the acquired optimal positions are used as the initial positions of CS and the CS is run until meets the terminal condition. The pseudo code of CS-PSO is as below.

Objective Function $f(x)$, $X = (x_1,...,x_d)^T$

Initialize the population of n particle swarm x_i

While (t<Max number of iterations)
  Evaluate every particle's fitness.
Get particle's local position and global position by PSO
algorithm.
Using particle's local position and global position as
initial population and get the new local position and
global position by CS algorithm
end while
Keep the global best solution

4 The Proposed CS_PSO Based SVM Model

4.1 The Idea of SVM Parameters Optimization

The performance of SVM mainly referred to the generalization ability. The penalty factor c and kernel function parameters σ exert a considerable influence on the generalization ability of SVM. The paper proposes to adopt CS_PSO algorithm to optimize parameters automatically. The main idea of applying CS_PSO to tune the best parameters pair (C and σ) of SVM is as following.

Each position vector of the CS_PSO stands for a candidate parameters pair for SVM. The initial population is generated with N number of solutions and each solution is a D-dimension vector, here D is set as 2 that each solution represents 2 parameters. x_i is the i-th particle position in the population which denotes a candidate parameter pair and its fitness can be measured by predefined fitness function, with the defined movement rules, the algorithm will run and until it terminates and output the best position as the optimal parameters for SVM.

4.2 Objective Function for Parameter Optimization

The goal of optimizing parameters for SVM is to utilize optimized procedures that explore a finite subset of the possible values to find the parameters that minimize the generalization error or maximize the correct classification rate. Thus, in the paper, the objective function of parameter optimization for SVM is the correct classification rate on the training data set.

4.3 The Implementation of the Proposed Method

The processes of the proposed CS_SPO for SVM parameters method are as follow, which mainly could be divided into 2 parts [21].

1. Direct Use of SVM

RBF kernel function is taken as kernel function in the paper. After the relevant parameters have been selected, RBF kernel function could be applied to any distribution of samples. The generalization ability of SVM algorithm is largely dependent on a set of parameters. The parameters needs to optimized are: RBF kernel parameter and the estimated accuracy. The n-fold approach is used to estimate the generalization ability. The data set was randomly divided into a one-second of a set (training set) and one-second of a set (testing set). The basic step is as follows [21]:

Step1. Input the sample training set, and set a group of parameters $\{c, \sigma\}$.
Step2. Train SVM based on the parameters. Calculate the cross validation error and obtains its object.
Step3. Test the SVM using object obtained from step 2.
Step4. Repeat the above step 25 times and find the average testing accuracy.

2. The proposed CS_PSO based SVM model

The procedure for describing proposed CS-PSO_SVM is as follows:

Step1. Initialize population size, inertia weight of PSO and parameters of CS and PSO,

Step2. Train SVM on particles.

Step3. Evaluate each particle's fitness value. Take the cross validation error of the SVM training set as fitness value.

Step4. Compare the fitness values and calculates the local optimal solution and global optimal solution.

Step5. Update the velocity and position of the each particle by Eqs. (16–17)

Step6. Take the local optimal solution and global optimal solution as the initial nest in cuckoo search.

Step7. Train SVM on nest.

Step8. Evaluate each nest's fitness value. Take the cross validation error of the SVM training set as fitness value.

Step9. Compare the fitness values and calculates the local optimal solution and global optimal solution.

Step10. Update the position of nest by Eqs. (18–19)

Step11. Repeat the step 2–10 until fitness function converges or the maximal number of iteration is reached.

Step12. The global best solution is input into SVM for classification.

5 Experimental Evaluation and Discussion

To show effectiveness of the proposed method, some real campus P2P traffic are used to evaluate the performance of the proposed CS-PSO based SVM for traffic identification of P2P; moreover, the performance is compared with some well known algorithms, that is GA-SVM, PSO-SVM. Moreover, the proposed method is compared with CS_SVM too. The main parameters used for these approaches are: the initial population for four algorithms is the same, that is 20, and all these algorithms will terminate after being executed 50 times. Moreover, the crossover rate for GA is 0.4 and mutation rate for GA is 0.01. And for PSO, $C_1 = 1.5$ and $C_2 = 1.7$, the value of inertia weight is set as 1. For CS, Pa = 0.25.

5.1 Data for Experiment

The base truth datasets were established manually from campus network. It was obtained from several host running P2P applications and several host running non-P2P applications. This experiment uses nearly 1386 samples, half of the samples are training set and the rest is testing set. P2P sample is positive class while non-P2P sample is negative, there are 968 positive samples and 418 negative samples.

5.2 P2P Traffic Features and Preprocessing

8 features are extracted and used in the paper, which are listed out as following, the time stamp, the time interval, the instantaneous flow rate, the packet length, time period, source port, destination port, the average flow rate per second. As is known that normalization is particularly useful for classification algorithms based on distance measurements, therefore, after collecting network traffic, we have used Min-max normalization to perform a linear transformation on the original data. Assume that *minA* and *maxA* are the minimum and maximum values of an attribute *A*. Min-max normalization maps a value, *v*, of *A* to *v'* in the range [*new_minA*; *new_maxA*] by computing (20).

$$v' = \frac{v - \min_A}{\max_A - \min_A}(new\_\max_A - new\_\min_A) + new\_\min_A \tag{20}$$

5.3 The Methods of Classification Evaluation

In order to test and evaluate the algorithms, the k-fold validation is adopted in the paper. That is, the data are divided into k subsets of approximately equal size. Each time, one of the k subsets is used as the test set and the other k-1 subsets form the training set. Performance statistics are calculated across all k trials. This provides a good indication of how well the classifier will perform on unseen data. In this experiment, k is set as 5. We have used the following quantity of result evaluation.

$$Identification\ Rate = \frac{T_P + T_N}{T_P + T_N + F_P + F_N} \tag{21}$$

The meaning of parameters in (21) is as below. T_P (True Positive): In case of test sample is positive and it is identified as positive, it is considered as a true positive; T_N (True Negative): in case of test sample is negative and it is identified as negative, it is considered as a true negative. FP (False Positive), in case of test sample is negative and it is identified as positive, it is considered as a false positive. FN (False Negative) in case of test sample is positive and it is identified as negative, it is considered as a false negative. The aim of any classification technique is to maximize the number of correct classification given by True Positive samples (TP) and True Negative samples (TN), whereas minimizing the wrong classification given by False Positive (FP) and False Negative (FN).

The range of parameters C and σ is from 2^{-10} to 2^{10} on the dataset. For these methods are stochastic algorithms all these methods have been run 30 times in order to make the results more reliable and impartial. Accuracy results of identification of 30 times are summarized in Table 1. Furthermore, some typical convergence procedures of these methods are displayed in Figs. 2, 3, 4 and 5.

In Table 1, BestAcc stands for the highest accuracy in 30 times test, WorstAcc is the lowest accuracy in 30 times test, and the average accuracy of 30 times test is expressed with AverAcc. According to Table 1, it is observed the proposed CS-PSO

Table 1. Running results with four approaches by 30 time

Approach	BestAcc	WorstAcc	AverAcc
GA + SVM	84.4156	81.3531	83.05918
CS + SVM	84.8485	80.8081	82.80906
PSO + SVM	84.7042	82.1068	83.46803
Proposed	85.2814	82.5397	83.78549

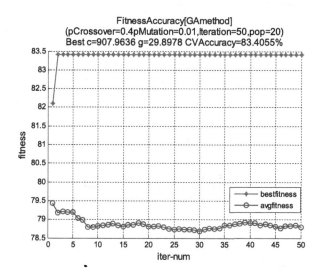

Fig. 2. Classified by GA based SVM

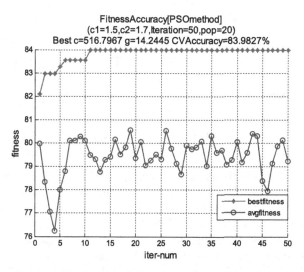

Fig. 3. Classified by PSO based SVM

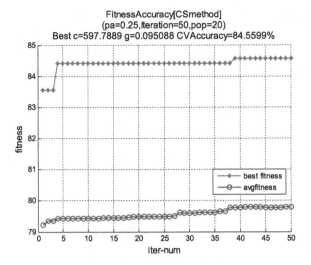

Fig. 4. Classified by CS based SVM

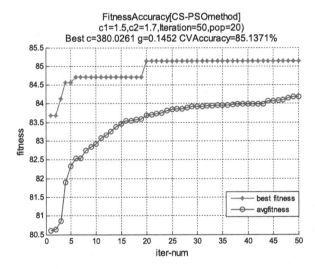

Fig. 5. Classified by CS-PSO based SVM

based SVM outperforms the other methods in all these data. It has the optimal BestAcc, WorstAcc and AverAcc. For example as for the highest accuracy, the CS-PSO based SVM is 85.2814 %, at the same time, the highest accuracy of the rest methods is less than 85 %; moreover, the CS-PSO based SVM has the highest average accuracy among these methods. It demonstrates that the performance of the proposed CS-PSO based SVM model is superior to GA-SVM, PSO-SVM and CS-SVM. Further, It is worth noting that as for the bestACC, the CS based SVM is better than PSO and GA based SVM but inferior to CS_PSO, because the terminal condition of the paper is max iteration and which is set only 50, as a result, though it could obtain fair good bestACC, its average correct rate is less than GA and PSO. Hence, by combining with PSO, the hybrid algorithm takes advantages of both PSO and CS, which could have a good balance of search efficiency and time consuming. Furthermore, Figs. 2, 3, 4 and 5 display that convergence rate of GA-SVM and PSO-SVM, which is very fast, CS is rather slow, in later of iteration, the best fitness of GA and PSO is almost no longer improved. Meanwhile, the best fitness of the proposed approach increases along with iterations, it illustrates that CS-PSO could avoid local optimal solution at the most extent. Lastly, the average fitness of CS-PSO is higher than other algorithm, it illustrates that performance of CS-PSO based SVM is more robust than GA based SVM, CS based SVM and PSO based SVM, which is more suitable for tuning parameters of SVM and P2P traffic identification.

6   Conclusion

In sum, a P2P traffic identification approach is developed based on SVM and CS_PSO in the paper. That is, for obtaining good tuning parameters of SVM, a CS_PSO method which combines Cuckoo Search algorithm and Particle Swarm Optimization algorithm is employed for parameter optimization of SVM. The proposed approach has been test on P2P dataset and compared with several existing approaches such as GA and PSO based SVM. The experimental results indicate that the proposed CS_PSO algorithm outperforms GA, PSO and CS based SVM and is feasible to optimize the parameters for SVM, which confirms that the new CS_PSO based SVM model can obtain ideal results. The schema is generic in identifying P2P applications. Our future work is to extend our approach to distinguish different P2P application flows by using ensemble learning SVM.

Acknowledgment. This work is supported by Natural Science Foundation of China (No. 41301371, 61170135 and 61202287), the Emergency Management Program for National Natural Science Foundation of China (No. 61440024), Doctor Fund of Hubei University of technology (BSQD13081 BSQD12032).

References

1. Steinmetz, R., Wehrle, K.: Peer-to-Peer Systems and Applications. Springer, Berlin (2005)
2. http://en.wikipedia.org/wiki/Peer-to-peer
3. Constantinou, F., Mavrommatis, P.: Identifying known and unkonwn peer-to-peer traffic. In: Fifth IEEE International Symposium on Network Computing and Application, pp. 93–102. IEEE Press, Cambridge, MA (2006)
4. Kim, M.-S., Kang, H.-J., Hong, J.W.: Towards Peer-to-Peer Traffic Analysis Using Flows. In: Brunner, Marcus, Keller, Alexander (eds.) DSOM 2003. LNCS, vol. 2867, pp. 55–67. Springer, Heidelberg (2003)
5. Bleul, H., Rathgeb, E.P.: A Simple, efficient, and flexible approach to measure multi-protocol peer-to-peer traffic. In: Lorenz, P., Dini, P. (eds.) Networking - ICN 2005. LNCS, vol. 3427. Springer, Heidelberg, pp. 606–616 (2005)

6. Sen, S., Spatscheck, O., Wang, D.: Accurate, scalable in-network identification of P2P traffic using application signatures. In: WWW2004, pp. 512–521. ACM Press, New York (2004)
7. Won, Y.J., Park, B.-C, Ju, H.-T.: A hybrid approach for accurate application traffic identification. In: 4th IEEE/IFIP Workshop on End-to-End Monitoring Techniques and Services, 2006, pp. 1–8. IEEE Press, Canada (2006)
8. Xu, K., Zhang, M., Ye, M., Chiu, D.M., Wu, J.: Identify P2P traffic by inspecting data transfer behavior. Comput. Commun. **33**, 1141–1150 (2010)
9. Keralapura, R., Nucci, A., Chuah, C.N.: A novel self-learning architecture for P2P traffic classification in high speed networks. Comput. Netw. **54**, 1055–1068 (2010)
10. Liu, B.: A semi-supervised clustering approach for P2P traffic classification. J. Netw. **6**(3), 424–431 (2011)
11. Moore, A.W., Zuev, D.: Internet traffic classification using Bayesian analysis techniques. In: Proceedings of ACM Sigmetrics, pp. 50–60 (2005)
12. Jin, F., Duan, Y.: A P2P flow identification model based on Bayesian network. In: 7th International Conference Wireless Communications, Networking and Mobile Computing (WiCOM), 2011, pp. 1–4. IEEE Press, Wuhan (2011)
13. Chen, H., Hu, Z., Ye, Z.:. Research of P2P traffic identification based on neural network. In: IEEE Conference on Computer Network and Multimedia Technology, 2009, pp. 18–20. IEEE Press, Wuhan (2009)
14. Chen, H., Zhou, X., You, F., Xu, H., Wang, C., et al.: A SVM approach for P2P traffic identification based on multiple traffic mode. J. Netw. **5**(11), 1381–1388 (2010)
15. Zheng, J., Xu, Y.: Identification of network traffic based on support vector machine. In: 2010 3rd International Conference on Advanced Computer Theory and Engineering, pp. 286–291. IEEE Press, Chengdu (2010)
16. VapNik, V.N.: The Nature of Statistical Learning Theory. Springer, New York (1995)
17. Eberhart, R.C., Shi, Y.: Comparison between genetic algorithms and particle swarm optimization. In: Proceedings of 1998 7th Annual Conference on Evoluationary Programming, vol. 1447, pp. 611–616. Springer, Berlin, Heidelberg (1998)
18. Kennedy, J., Eberhart, R.: Particle swarm optimization. In: Proceedings of IEEE International Conference on Neural Networks, 1995, pp. 1942–1948. IEEE Press, Piscataway (1995)
19. Esmin, A., Torres, G., Zambroni, A.: A hybrid particle swarm optimization applied to loss power minimization. IEEE Trans. Power Syst. **20**(2), 859–866 (2005)
20. Ting, T.O.: A novel approach for unit commitment problem via an effective hybrid particle swarm optimization. IEEE Trans. Power Syst. **21**(1), 11–418 (2006)
21. Parimala, R.: Feature selection using a novel particle swarm optimization and It's variants. I. J. Inf. Technol. Comput. Sci. **5**, 16–24 (2012)
22. Yang, X., Deb, S.: Cuckoo search via levy fights. In: 2009 World Congress on Nature and Biologically Inspired Computing (NaBIC 2009), India, pp. 210–215. IEEE Press, Coimbatore (2009)
23. Civicioglu, P., Besdok, E.: A conceptual comparison of the cuckoo-search, particle swarm optimization, differential evolution and artificial bee colony algorithms. Artif. Intell. Rev. **39**, 315–346 (2013)
24. Wang, F., Luo, L., He, X., Wang, Y.: Hybird optimization algorithm of PSO and Cickoo search. In: IEEE 2011 2nd International Conference on Artificial Intelligence, Management Science and Electronic Commerce (AIMSEC), pp. 1172–1175. IEEE Press, Deng Leng (2011)
25. http://en.wikipedia.org/wiki/Support_vector_machine
26. Boser, B.E., Guyon, I.M., Vapnik, V.N.: A training algorithm for optimal margin classifiers. In: 5th Annual ACM Workshop on COLT, pp. 144–152. ACM Press, New York (1992)

Author Index

Printed in the United States
By Bookmasters